Surviving Your Split
A Guide to Healing and Hope after Your Divorce
By: Dr. Nicolya Williams

Surviving Your Split
A Guide to Healing and Hope after Your Divorce
By: Dr. Nicolya Williams
Copyright 2020 Clarity Cove Publishing
ISBN: 978-1-948985-03-1
All Rights Reserved. No part of this book can be scanned, distributed or copied without permission.
Cover Art by Sam Designs
Interior Design by Nicolya Williams

Table of Contents

Acknowledgments..4

Introduction...7

Stages of Divorce..9

Surviving the split..18

Taking action...30

How do I build resilience?....................................34

How to get revenge on your ex............................39

Overcoming Infidelity...45

Getting through the special days while hurting....51

How to talk to your children about divorce...........56

How to co-parent effectively................................62

How to handle bad mouthing...............................68

Getting help legally..73

Forgiveness...77

Embracing Change..81

Below the surface..85

Conquering your mind..89

Setting goals for your future self..........................96

Redefining who you are.....................................102

Self-love...106

Conclusion...116

BONUS Self-care review...............................120

Acknowledgments

To my Lord and Savior: You are omnipotent, almighty and powerful. Thank you for fighting for me, for loving me and for turning everything around for my good. I could never thank you enough. Crazy to believe that I am here sharing this part of my story. Thank you for allowing my test to be a testament of who You are and who I am in You. I am Your child and for that I am forever grateful. I love and honor you.

Kaelyn: When I first held you in my arms, I knew I would love you forever. I was just a baby myself when I had you, but I thank God daily that you were sent to me. When you came into my life, it made me work to be the best mommy I could be. Every day you encourage me to go after my goals. Every day you pray for me. Every day I learn something from you. Thank you for just being you. I am so grateful that I have a daughter as honest, beautiful, and intelligent as you. I hope you realize that you are unbelievably precious to me, I love you more and more each day.

Kamryn: I knew it was a blessing to have a child, but I had no idea how much my life would change when you were born. I feel like I blinked and time flew by. It seems like yesterday you were learning how to crawl, then walk, and now you are running. I am so proud of the phenomenal person you have become. Thank you for showing me how wonderful being a parent is. Every day your determination inspires me, your curiosity emboldens me, and your love warms me. I don't know how such a small little girl can generate so much energy, but I do know how you create so much happiness in my life: By being YOU! I love you baby and know that each day my love grows more.

To my dear Auntie Gay. Thank you for always believing in my writing and supporting it through the good, bad, ugly and beautiful. I am beyond blessed to have you in my corner. I love you so much!

This book is dedicated to everyone who desires to make this next chapter the best chapter…

Your thoughts and actions can transform any situation into either an obstacle or an opportunity.....

There are seasons in life when we get lost, stuck or overwhelmed. It can be extremely challenging to see going through a divorce as a "new opportunity."

I get it.

But the truth is, there are many changes that come with a divorce and those changes open a lot of new opportunities

As women, we often feel powerless when going through the process of divorce. It can feel like you are losing control and that life makes no sense

But you are POWERFUL! More than you can even know or imagine

I may sound crazy, but what I do know is that you have the POWER to heal your hurt.

You have the POWER to start again, better than before.

If you believe that you're powerless and that the divorce is happening to you, your actions will match this belief.

If on the other hand you believe that the divorce is happening FOR you and to your benefit, your actions will match this belief

I am passionate about helping you get out of a broken state of mind and truly heal.

I was stuck for a long time and it was a terrible state of being.... I want more for you!

You matter.

Your mind matters.

Your life matters.

It's time for you to act as such.

Introduction

"You can and will survive this. Do not let your reality tell you any different."
~Dr. Nicolya

When I asked for a divorce, I didn't think it through. I didn't think about the financial impact it would have on me. I didn't think about how it would hurt my children. I didn't think about the perceived generational curse I continued with my family. I didn't even think of all of the years and time I had fought for us to be together. I just wanted the pain to end and getting out seemed to be the only answer.

I will never forget the night I sent a text message saying "I am done." I didn't want to talk face to face for fear that he would try to change my mind. The truth was I still loved him, but I knew he didn't love me and I knew this wasn't healthy for anyone. So I sent the text, changed the locks and filed for divorce. Before court, I began planning how we would make time for him to see our daughters and I only talked to him regarding our children. Of course he tried to discuss more but I just wanted to be done.

I thought that it would be simple to just file and sign, especially since it didn't appear that we had anything to fight over. I was very wrong. About two months later while waiting for our first court date, I was served with an order that he was pursuing full custody. I went from hurt and sad to angry and panicky. None of those emotions are helpful when you have to make decisions.

I'll save you all the gritty details but we proceeded to fight for 18 long months in court and I alone spent over $30,000 in legal fees. Looking back, I wish I knew what to expect and what I would feel. I wish I knew that it was okay not to be okay. I wish I knew it was okay to get support. I wish I knew it was helpful to talk to people who had blazed the trail before me. If you're reading this, I want you to know these things. It is the reason I wrote this book.

I wrote this book to encourage and support not only those going through a divorce, but also those in the midst of a split, whether that be from a bad breakup, or your "everythingship" ending. While you may see me reference marriage throughout this book, I do recognize that breaking up after an intense or lengthy relationship can be extremely painful as well.

Each healing process is unique. Whatever you're thinking, feeling and experiencing is okay. Also understand that what you're thinking, feeling and experiencing won't always be what you're thinking and feeling. There will be smiling again. There will be happiness again. There will be love again. There will be life again.

Stages of Divorce
"When two people decide to get a divorce, it isn't a sign that they don't understand one another. But it is a sign that they have at least begun to."
- Helen Rowland

When we think about grief and loss, we usually think about death. Grief is a psychological response to loss, characterized by sadness, yearning, and even obsessive remembrance of the person or thing that is gone. The death of someone close is impactful, but research shows that going through a divorce is comparable to experiencing a death. There are many reasons people grieve. Some examples include losing a job, the death of a pet, miscarriage and stillbirth, severed friendships, serious illness or major financial mishaps. While loss is universal, the experience of grief is unique to each individual. The experience of grief changes based on culture, personality, and even the circumstances surrounding the loss, among other things. In other words, there is no "correct" way to grieve. I have noticed that potential clients get concerned that they have to follow a certain plan to rid themselves of the pain, but I make a concerted effort to ensure they understand that there is no correct way to "do divorce".

Sadly, love lasts much longer than the split. When you lose someone you love, you are never really "done" with grief. You will love and remember the people you care about throughout your life. However, the intensity of grief does change over time. While everyone moves through grief differently, psychologist Elizabeth Kubler-Ross has identified five stages that many people experience. In working through my own process, I have come to see that these stages are pretty spot on.

Although these "stages" have been identified, the process in which the stages unfold may not be linear. In other words, you may not move from stage one to five in that order. Also, you may not experience each stage for the same length of time. The reality is that splitting up looks different for each party in the relationship, but this is normal. Reactions, beliefs and the steps taken after the split are based on perspectives and beliefs not only about the relationship, but about each individual in the relationship.

As the denial wears off, reality slowly sinks in until it becomes too much and denial takes over again. This process helps to serve grief in doses we can manage. After the first days or weeks of loss, however, refusing to accept reality can hinder the healing process. Ultimately, the only way to deal with the pain is to go through it. You must allow yourself to feel it.

The first stage is denial and shock. In the early stages of

grief, it's normal to deny the reality of what's happening. We think that the divorce or separation must somehow be a mistake. The denial and shock actually serves as a protective function. Because losing someone can cause overwhelming pain, denying this reality can be a temporary way to calm the pain.

The second stage is anger. When we experience loss, anger can be overwhelming. It's normal and natural to feel rage. Your anger may have many targets: God, the universe, your ex, your ex's family, or yourself. It's ok to feel that rage. Only by feeling your anger can you dissipate its force. Many people believe that anger is a bad emotion, but the truth is that it's simply an emotion. How we handle it determines whether it is good or bad.

The third stage is bargaining. In grief, it's common to be tormented by "what-if" statements such as, "What if I tried harder?" or, "What if we had gone to counseling sooner?" These what-if statements are often accompanied by guilt for not having done something differently so as to prevent the loss. These thoughts are a form of bargaining with a higher power. "If only" something could be different, everything would be okay again. I toyed with these questions for quite some time, but as a Christian, I learned to embrace the reality that everything does indeed work together for the good of those who love the Lord and are called according to His purpose. Now, understand that things may not feel like they are working together for your good as you go through your experience. It will be painful and likely will make no sense. Understand though that bargaining keeps you in a stagnant place. The reality is that no matter how much you attempt to change the past by overthinking it, it won't change. So we should not be putting our focus on the past, but instead on the present which is the only thing we can make choices to start changing.

Depression is the fourth stage. Depression is categorized as a mental health disorder where you lose interest in activities you once enjoyed. You will know you're depressed if you struggle with liking things you once loved, you experience a lack of motivation or constantly feel down. Depression impacts the way you feel, think and act. The reality is that as loss sinks in, you can experience an overwhelming sense of sadness. You may even find yourself yearning for your ex, plans that were made, or fantasies of what could have been. This stage is tough, because the darkness that ensues can be overwhelming, if you're not getting the support that you need. Don't delay in getting help. Most people are unable or unwilling to get support then. I refer to the stage of depression as the final hump. It is the hardest stage for most people to break out of, but when you move out of it you're able to move forward with acceptance.

The fifth stage is acceptance: As your level of acceptance increases, the pain will diminish. Understand that acceptance does not indicate that you are forgetting what has happened, and it certainly isn't evidence that you've forgotten about what transpired. It simply exhibits your understanding and acknowledgement of said events in order to move forward. While the situation is part of your story, it no longer takes over your life.

Often, these five steps are presented as a checklist. There is no default way to experience grief. Divorce is an experience that causes people to mourn. The process of healing and mourning looks different for each individual. Although these five steps are common, they are not universal. They are intended to assist people with understanding some of the emotions they may experience. I often see clients cycle through these steps multiple times before ending at acceptance. For example, they may go from bargaining to depression back to bargaining and then acceptance. In order to ensure you're not cycling through these stages over and over again, it is beneficial to evaluate your healing process to avoid the chance of putting on a façade. Many people try to improve their outer appearance, but fail to tackle the root of the problem. You have to break free by making wholeness your priority.

During the grieving process, you can experience other symptoms. These could be symptoms that affect you physically such as nausea, stomach pain, loss of appetite, sleeping too much or insomnia, headaches, and aches and pains. These symptoms can cause depression which can ultimately result in an individual not wanting to get out of bed each day. Some studies suggest that after a divorce, some people will experience broken heart syndrome. A person will experience heart attack symptoms including chest pain, shortness of breath, and even heart failure. Our bodies process both physical pain and social pain through the same pathways in the body as emotional pain. In other words, emotional pain hurts physically, in the same way that physical pain does. It is imperative to exercise self-care during this time.

After a divorce, the grief process may cause you to deal with emotions such as: sadness, anger, confusion, fear, regret, guilt, and shame. This mix of emotions can be complicated, and people sometimes feel an extra measure of guilt and shame about where they are in life or how things transpired. Throughout the divorce process, there is no correct set of emotions that you are guaranteed to feel or even required to feel. Outwardly, you may be angry and experience fits of rage. Or, you could become withdrawn and cry privately. Each response is valid. It is okay to go through your process however you see fit as long as your reactions aren't hurting yourself or others. Your job is to acknowledge that you feel the emotions and then learn from them as you move forward.

Sadly, some people do make choices that are hurtful. If you are going through a separation or divorce, there are some choices that may feel good in the moment, but have negative repercussions. I'd like to go over a few things you should avoid.

- **Drugs and alcohol** can be a tempting indulgence in an effort to self-medicate. However, experiencing the emotions that come along with grief is the only way to process and ultimately tackle the emotions that are holding you hostage. Drugs and alcohol don't make the pain go away, they just numb it and even that is temporary. The pain will be right there waiting for you when you become sober again. You are also more like to engage in behavior and activities that are risky and detrimental to the wellbeing of yourself and those around you. Because alcohol is a depressant, you're more like to actually experience depression once you're sober again, in spite of the fact that it makes you feel good in the moment.
- **Making major life decisions** is another thing that should be avoided. Living with the pain can make it easy to imagine that everything would be different if you move, change jobs, or make other major changes. The truth is, it's difficult to make good decisions in the midst of grief because it often causes fear, confusion, anxiety and exhaustion. These emotions are a never a good place to be in when it comes to making life decisions. I recognize that some decisions are required to be made as a result of going

through divorce. For example, moving may be necessary as a result of the house that was shared with your former spouse needing to be sold. Be sure to seek wise and/or legal counsel to ensure you make the best decision possible. You don't want to make any decision out of emotion only to have to deal with repercussions of those decisions later.

- **Avoid trying to be busy all the time**. This was a big one for me during my divorce. I buried myself with my business, extracurricular activities with my children, and pretty much anything that could get my mind off of the situation. It is possible to use these things to push grief away, but understand that the pain will still be there when you slow down. Sometimes, putting grief aside to focus on other things is necessary. For example, you still need to pay rent, feed the kids, and go to work. The short breaks from grief to take care of these things can prevent you from becoming overwhelmed. But do not be fooled into believing that you should be consistently pushing those tough feelings to the side. Always take time to sit with your emotions, reflect and meditate. Allow yourself to learn from what you're experiencing and feeling. I firmly believe that our emotions are feedback. Our emotions teach us about who we are, what we are feeling, and what we need. We have to be able to exist with these emotions to not only heal, but to grow. This is how we grow through what we go through.
- **Don't neglect yourself**. Grief is exhausting and it can be easy to neglect your self-care routine. It is imperative that you continue taking care of yourself. You don't have to keep a perfect house and cook three-course meals, but you need to shower, eat, move your body, and take care of basic daily tasks. Take care of yourself the way you would take care of your best friend in their time of grief. Ultimately, you matter just as much. More importantly, you can't be good to anyone else if you're not good to yourself first.

Overall grief is difficult to process and face. The truth is if you continue to avoid it, it doesn't prevent you from having to address it, it just delays the inevitable. Do not try to run from the pain. Understand that there is a lot that can be learned during this time. I tell my clients all the time, and I live by this truth- triggers and pain are the biggest teacher.

In high school I lost my best friend, Jessica, in a very traumatic way. I remember the day I found out as I was working at TJ Maxx n' More. A mutual friend of ours called me and I stormed out of work. I was devastated. I felt like I couldn't even see straight or think straight and I was praying that it was just a bad dream. When I got in my car there was an Adina Howard song playing. I'm not sure if you know anything about Adina Howard but she doesn't have sad or sappy songs. They are mostly sexual in nature.

Because of what was happening in the moment, that song stuck with me for years to come. I couldn't even listen to the beginning beat without breaking down. For years, I avoided listening to that song, or really anything similar because it was too painful. Well, I later came to learn that the song was a trigger for me. That song triggered that exact moment and emotional state every time it played. Now, to be clear, there is nothing wrong with the song itself. The fact is, I hadn't healed from the emotions I experienced from the loss I experienced that day. I have since tried to be more in tune with my emotional triggers. We all have them.

It's much like your marriage and your divorce. After it's over, some people are triggered by talking about relationships, or going to weddings etc. You could even have specific triggers, like driving past the restaurant where you caught your ex cheating. The problem is, most people run from their triggers because addressing them is extremely painful and overwhelming. However, denying their existence or hiding from them is just delaying the healing that need to take place. Your triggers will continue to control you until they are addressed. Triggers are not bad; in fact they can be our greatest teachers if we allow them to be.

A trigger is an unhealed emotional wound. In reality, triggers happen to us all- but they look different for each person and situation. It's tempting to avoid triggers because addressing them hurts and it is hard work. But if you don't work through your triggers they will haunt you. It will impact you at work, at home and personally.

I am a firm believer that triggers serve as a teacher for the areas in our life that need healing. Triggers are not bad, they actually give us the opportunity to observe and reflect which enables healing. I tell my clients often that there is so much wisdom in our wounds, but if we try to cover them up or hide them, we aren't allowing that space to learn. Triggers can help you to learn about yourself, as well as assist you in building your resilience. And trust me resilience is a skill you definitely want to have.

Many people don't know where to begin with healing those deep wounds that prevent triggers. That is what I would like to share with you. Please understand that the process is not simple. If it were, everyone would be doing it. It can be challenging at times, but without truly healing your triggers they will control you. Being controlled by triggers is not healthy. The work that you will put into addressing your triggers and healing them will literally change your life.

The first step is to identify your trigger and the reason it exists. This is probably the most difficult step because it's tempting to want to flee when you begin to feel triggered. I challenge you to be still and notice what emotions you're feeling when it happens. Identify what situations, people, places or things trigger those emotions and consider where you think those events are rooted. Sometimes when you dig deep the root may be surprising to you. The quicker you notice an emotion is triggered, the sooner you can discover if the threat is real or not. You can also create a plan for how to handle it when and if it comes up again.

The second step is to accept responsibility for your reactions. You have more power than you can ever imagine, but if you play victim you will remain a victim. Take time to ask yourself what your life would look like if you were in control of your reactions.
The more you practice working through the difficult emotions the more you can begin to shift your beliefs about them and the impact they have in your life. Also, when you accept responsibility for your actions you can move to the second part of choosing how you want to feel and react moving forward. When you seek to shift your perspective as well as your emotions, you gain emotional freedom, which is priceless. It is exhausting to lead a life led by emotions.

The third step is to determine what you need. This is important because I think that we run so far from our triggers and our problems that we're not even in touch with what we need for true healing. We cover our pain with people, drugs, alcohol, and being busy, etc. Ask yourself whether you need time, love, support or to make sense of the situation. Do you need to forgive yourself? Do you need to be still? If you sit with yourself for long enough, your body will not steer you wrong. You will also be more in touch with what it is you need in the moment. Your body will let you know what you need but you have to be patient with the process. Also note that needs are NOT bad. They are what will serve you through this process.

    The fourth and final step is to get support. Many times there's a lot of stigma about having to share your "problems" or having to get support, but I'm here to share that getting support is the very thing that may change your life. Triggers often come from traumatic experiences which are difficult to not only discuss but overcome. You wouldn't trust yourself to pull out your own tooth so don't trust yourself to pull up those deep wounds alone. It's also helpful when you start to dig up those deep wounds to have someone there to encourage support and motivate and hold you accountable on the journey. Don't allow cultural stigmas to keep you stuck in shame.

Surviving the split
"Don't allow yourself to fall victim to regret. You can find wisdom beneath your wounds."
-Dr. Nicolya

According to the most recent statistics, approximately 42% of first-time marriages end in divorce, 60% of second marriages end in divorce and 73% of third marriages end in divorce. In the United States, it is estimated that there is approximately one divorce taking place every 35 seconds. This equates to 2,400 divorces in one day. That only applies to the *United States*. Studies also show that the first year of marriage is the most difficult because this is when you're getting to know an individual. Therefore, about 70% of breakups happen within the first year and if you can make it to the five-year mark, you're increasing your likelihood of marriage. I am not sharing that to scare you or guilt trip you, but to arm you with information and remind you that you're not alone.

You are probably reading this book because you've gone through a nasty split, a difficult divorce, or a hard breakup. Life after a split can be a challenge. Some people do well. They are able to move forward and redefine their life, including transforming on a personal level. On the other hand, some people struggle to redefine who they are. They struggle to make sense of the situation. They struggle with tough emotions and feel like a failure.

The difference between those individuals has nothing to do with time or money. It has everything to do with mindset. The biggest difference between those who are able to bid farewell to the failed marriage or relationship and those who don't is whether they believe they deserve to stay stuck in a negative state. Take a moment and ask yourself:

Do I deserve to struggle?
Am I the victim?
Do I feel sorry for myself?
OR
Do I deserve happiness?
Do I deserve a fresh start?
Do I believe I deserve the things I desire?

If you strongly believe that you deserve happiness and that fresh beginning, you can bid farewell more easily. But if you decide that a terrible thing happened to you, that you deserve to be a victim, and everyone should feel sorry for you, you will remain stuck and it will continue to be a difficult journey.

I've worked with clients who are ten years out of a bad breakup or eight years past the divorce and they're still angry, bitter and stuck. The reason why people get stuck is because it's familiar and comfortable. They normalize playing the victim or being angry and bitter. They are accustomed to the same routine, the same frustrations and have allowed themselves to stay stuck in those thought patterns. This is never a good thing. Allowing yourself to be stuck isn't okay whether it's a relationship, job or a business. The only thing constant in the world is change. When you learn to embrace change and allow it to work in your favor, success and happiness will be yours.

A while back, I read an awesome book called *Operation Happiness*. The premise of the book is that happiness is a decision, but we often allow external factors to determine whether we're allowed to be happy or not. It is okay to be happy and we have permission to be happy, we just need to give that permission to ourselves. Happiness is a mindset belief. It is not based on who you're married to or what happened to you. It's not even based on how much money you have. It's literally a choice; A daily choice to wake up happy and work to be happy. When I learned that, it changed my life.

I went through an incredibly difficult divorce a few years ago. We have two children, so maintaining a relationship with my ex was very difficult. For a long time, I was angry at God. I was angry at my ex. I was angry with myself. I was mad at the whole world, honestly. I looked to blame everyone for my divorce. I was angry because ultimately I believe that although I did my best, I couldn't understand how it ended up so bad, so contentious and downright painful. I mean it literally felt like part of my body was being detached. For what seemed like forever, I stayed stuck, angry, sad, hurt and frustrated. I allowed myself to possess the mindset of a victim. I allowed shame to take over my life and distance myself from a lot of people as a result of the pain that I felt. I walked around so embarrassed because it almost felt as if the scarlet letter "D" was written on my forehead. I became consumed with the idea that divorce was part of my identity instead of one chapter in my story. It took me a long time to learn what I hope everyone knows: divorce does not determine who you are or even necessarily what you deserve.

After my experience, I promised myself that as much as I could help it, no woman would struggle to heal after divorce as long as they allowed me to help them. I wanted my story to be encouraging for other women. I wanted what was once an embarrassment to me to be the very thing that created breakthroughs for those who were struggling. Through my own experience I broke my healing into seven stages which I will share with you. Understand that this is not always easy and it's not always fun. There will be steps and decisions that are difficult, but the end result will be worth it.

Don't fight the feelings. Deal with whatever comes up. You can only push so much under the rug before it begins to show. Feel the feeling, process it and let yourself learn from it. Ignoring those feelings will not help. It may help temporarily, but in the long run it does not. This is how anxiety and depression manifests. It is the result of trying to stay strong without processing your true feelings. You may think that burying yourself with work going out to drink with friends or even entering into a new relationship will help, but the reality is that those tough feelings will show up. Sometimes it shows as depression or irritability, but it can also manifest in the way of you isolating yourself. You must begin healing the right way. Masking the pain will only cause more trauma in the long run.

Don't do it alone. Going through a divorce is drastic. Don't ever allow yourself to believe you're alone in what you're dealing with. The best thing you can do for yourself is find a support system. This may be through your church, a group of good friends, or hiring a counselor or a coach. A part of the challenge of going through a divorce is the cycle of emotions you will experience. Having a strong support system will help you to stay grounded. If possible, you want to avoid allowing your divorce to take over every aspect of your life. One thing to keep in mind is to make sure your support system is outside your place of employment. You need to focus on handling your duties on the job. This can also cause issues or frustration amongst your coworkers. Also, keep in mind that your children should not be your support. It is important that you keep boundaries for them and maintain a sense of normalcy through the transition.

I made a life changing decision during my divorce. I hired a life coach. It had become a challenge to encourage myself in the midst of dealing with so many tough decisions. I had a desire to follow a particular path and needed to get back on track. No matter who you choose to confide in during this time, be intentional about choosing someone with whom you can be transparent. You don't need a person who will allow you to sugarcoat your feelings or hide your hurts. You need someone who will allow you to be honest and vulnerable as you work through your healing process.

Next: Don't personalize the loss. This is where mindset comes into play. This could be where you begin to blame yourself for what happened and become consumed with negative thoughts and feelings. The truth is that life has ups and downs. There are some things that happen that make sense and other things that make no sense at all. The Bible says in Romans 8:28, "God works everything together for the good of those who love him and are called according to His purpose." I clung to this verse during my divorce process. I am a walking testament of those words.

As I was going through my divorce, I couldn't make sense of it or understand why it was happening. Although this was the case, people started inquiring how I was able to go through it with such dignity. They wanted to know how I recovered from it. I realized that the test was my testimony. I learned that there was a purpose behind my pain. I came to see that I would be able to share my experiences and encourage others as a result. I knew that I would be able to listen to others and empathize with them. I know firsthand what it feels like to sit in the pain and I know what it's like to find myself again after the loss. If I hadn't experienced the divorce, the loss and devastation, I wouldn't have this opportunity to impact the lives of the women around me. Ultimately, I was able to birth a business around what I consider to be the most embarrassing experience of my life.

Setting boundaries is also a critical component. This especially applies for those who overstep them. These boundaries can apply to your ex, but it does not have to stop there. The boundaries you implement can be for your children, family, friends, colleagues, etc. For example, if you're good friends with your former sister-in-law, it is okay to keep the friendship, but limit the conversations to things that don't have anything to do with the divorce or her brother.

If there are places that you and your ex may have frequented such as the barber shop or hair salon, you may encounter employees who ask questions. It's okay to pull back, change shops or let them know that you're grieving and need some space. It's not personal. You may encounter situations where you and your ex decide you want to be friends for the sake of your children, so he offers to help you by mowing your lawn in exchange for lunch prepared by you. It's okay to let him know that it's something you're not able to do because you're hurting. It's okay to revisit that down the line.

Another potential boundary that needs to be considered is how to handle when you miss your former mate and vice versa, especially if you know it's not healthy to communicate with them in that way. It's okay to miss that person but do they need to know that you miss them? Do you need to check their social media to see what they're doing? Boundaries are a form of protection, and you should implement them as necessary.

Boundaries should not only apply to others. Sometimes you will need to set boundaries for yourself. I remember shortly after my divorce; my brakes went out. I knew my ex was good at fixing brakes, but I also knew that reaching out to him would be emotionally painful for me. I decided that my car repairs from that point forward would be at an auto shop. Here are a few other "boundaries":

- I'm not going to vent to my kids about this.
- I'm not going to carry this baggage into work.
- I'm not going to allow myself to perseverate on what happened for more than ten minutes at a time.

These boundaries are important to your healing process. Do understand though, that your boundaries could look different from the examples I gave. You may be able to ask your ex-husband for assistance with car repairs and not struggle emotionally. That is wonderful. The goal is to set boundaries that you need to work through your healing process effectively.

If you don't set boundaries and expectation, you may experience a downward spiral. Once you take your personal business into work, you'll be stuck talking about it at work and now all the people at your job will know your business. Once you involve your children it can be difficult to undo the pain or confusion it may cause. Once you allow your ex back in your home for lunch on Saturdays, it may be tough to change when you begin dating again. Set boundaries and be willing to adjust as time goes on, but adjust to make sure it is supporting your healing, not adjusting to other's hurt feelings or manipulation.

I firmly believe that the only people that get bothered by boundaries are those who can't take advantage of you as a result of that boundary being set. You should have boundaries with pretty much everyone in your life. Not because of a divorce, but because it's a good practice to implement. Boundaries are an imperative part of self-care. You should have boundaries with your boss, boundaries with your children, boundaries with your parents, boundaries with your future significant other, and boundaries with your friends. You should have boundaries in every way in order to protect yourself, especially during a loss or a split. You're going to be dealing with a lot and you have to make sure to protect yourself during this process.

Having healthy boundaries is critical to getting through your divorce. Without healthy boundaries you can attract people into your life that do not mean well for you or you can trigger things that will prevent you from healing. Boundaries are things that we often have as children, but then as adults we forget the importance of implementing them. An example of a boundary that our parents give us is a bedtime. Children respond better when there are strict boundaries in place and as adults we forget this and then wonder why we struggle. When boundaries are in place life runs a lot smoother.

If you are new to setting boundaries, or make a decision to become intentional about setting them, it is helpful to create a practical approach to make them a part of your routine. The first step in creating boundaries is to consider your past. Think about what has worked for you and what has not. What people or places trigger difficult emotions? Where have you been taken for granted in your life? Identify boundaries that you can put in place to prevent the pitfalls from happening.

The second step is to identify the boundaries for each area of your life. The reason you will want to separate each individual area is because each one will have different boundaries. For example, a work boundary may be that you do not complete any work related tasks on the weekend. This same boundary cannot apply to your family, as you may be a parent and we all know that job does not stop on the weekend. The third step is to give yourself permission to accept and follow the boundaries you have listed. Fear and guilt are the two emotions people often feel when setting up boundaries. In order to challenge that guilt and fear list all of the benefits of setting these boundaries. Then make a list of what will happen if you don't put a boundary in place. Remember boundaries are for your peace.

The fourth step in setting boundaries is to make self-care a priority. There is a bonus assessment to help you with this. When you practice self-care you are putting yourself first. The truth is that you aren't good to anyone unless you are first good to yourself. The more you care for yourself the more you are able to recognize the importance of boundaries and why you deserve it. The fifth step is to take it one step at a time and start small. When setting boundaries, it is important that you do not overwhelm yourself. You have to become accustomed to having boundaries. Start with a small boundary that is not threatening to you and then build from there.

The sixth step to surviving your split is to hold tight to your faith. During the divorce process, do not allow circumstances to cause you to lose faith. It may be tempting, but this will keep you moving forward. It can be difficult to see that the future can be brighter than the past but never allow your past to inform your future. If you decide that because you had a nasty divorce, you're never getting married, you may miss out on love or happiness. If you decide that because your ex-husband was 5'8 you will never speak to another person who has the same height, you have no clue who you may miss out on knowing. My plea to you is to hold tight to your faith so that God can restore what you lost. I don't mean restore as in give you back the ex who treated you like trash and did things like degrade you and call you names. What I mean is that you can have an opportunity to find something new again in the future. You can start again and let the next chapter become the best chapter. Don't miss that opportunity.

Although your decision to marry may have felt like a bad decision, you can't allow that to determine the course of your life. It is important to glean from each experience then apply the wisdom and knowledge that you gain to future decisions. However, you must be careful not to make extreme or rash decisions as a result. You could say, "I will never live with a man again in my life…" but the reality is that the choice to do so could lead to love, marriage, children and happiness. Keep the faith because your future can be brighter than your past. You deserve to live your best life, no matter what happened. Own it.

The seventh step is to sharpen your saw, which comes from the book *The Seven Habits of Highly Effective People* by Dr. Stephen Covey. As a school counselor, I referenced the habit of sharpening your saw quite frequently as a result of being a big advocate for self-care. The premise in the book is that a guy was walking through a forest and saw a gentleman cutting down a tree. Although he was working diligently to cut down the tree, he wasn't making much progress. The man who was walking inquired on whether the saw needed to be sharpened. The gentleman responded that he didn't have time to, he was just focused on cutting the tree down. The man responded and told him that if he just took five minutes to sharpen the saw, he would save time and cut the tree down much more quickly. Wow! How powerful!

The same concept applies to your life. As women, we often wear multiple hats and we bear the responsibility of taking care of our children, working full time, running a business, catering to our significant other, volunteering at church, expecting to do all these things with ease and excitement. We often end up putting self-care on the backburner and get burned out. You can't be good to anyone if you're not first good to yourself. This phrase may seem to be overused, but I like to consider the "airplane phenomenon." About a year ago, I was on a flight to Paris with my daughters. As a part of the safety overview, the flight attendant explained that if there was some type of emergency and we needed to use the face masks, that we should secure out own face masks before helping someone around you. That may seem extreme for some, but the truth is if you don't put the mask on yourself it is guaranteed you won't be able to rescue anyone else including yourself.

If you don't first love yourself and take care of yourself, you're not going to effectively love or take care of anyone else. Taking care of yourself may mean you need to schedule a family vacation soon. It could also be as simple as taking the time to sit down and paint your nails, or read a great book you've been wanting to check out. Understand that you deserve it. The thing is, you have to be intentional about executing it. This is how you sharpen your saw and enable a more productive healing process.

The final step in this process is to celebrate the new you. I encourage my one-on-one clients to create some sort of celebration around the divorce or breakup. We often get sad when it happens, isolate, cry, lay in bed, eat ice cream, watch breakup movies and even listen to sad songs. Stop! You have to consider all the opportunities that you have in front of you with this life change. Your future needs you more than your past. Don't waste your time wallowing in self-pity. You must look towards the future and work towards the things you desire to have. Ask yourself, "How can I celebrate me?" That could mean to do something that your ex-husband was afraid to do, like taking a cruise, going to an Escape Room or zip lining. My ex-husband didn't love traveling, so traveling was always more like a burden. I always had a love for traveling but didn't go as much while married. Upon the completion of my divorce I took a trip to Cozumel, Mexico for my birthday. That was not to celebrate the divorce, but to celebrate a new beginning, to celebrate a new reality for me. I wanted to begin to make decisions that aligned with the future I desired.

What can you begin to do or create that will give you something to look forward to? Defining you may be new, and may take a lot of work and changes. Defining yourself can also change during the process as you learn more about yourself. There is going to be a lot of growth, personal development, and self-discovery. You're going to have to dig deep. You will also have to create new routines. As you disassociate from the life you had with your partner, you may discover things that you didn't realize were on autopilot.

Maybe every day you used to meet your ex at the gym at 4 o'clock. You may have to recreate routines that fit your single life. You could choose to make 4 o'clock your meditation time, or it could be a chance to go to happy hour with your coworkers. Changing these routines is healthy for you. Not only does it help you break the habits that you created, but it can give you something new to look forward to. This also gives you a chance to focus on something new instead of thinking of the past and becoming consumed in sadness.

During my divorce process I had a hard time with some of my former routines. I struggled with was checking my phone for the good morning text I would receive from my ex-husband after I got to work. I decided to share this with a good friend that was also going through a divorce. She mentioned that she also missed the good morning texts as well. We decided that we would send a simple "good morning" message to one another. That small change helped in big ways for both of us. Also, our constant communication allowed us to check in with each other regularly and it was a great way to continue supporting one another through a tough time. Over time as you create these new routines, you'll start to forget some of the things that you used to do. The hope is that the new routine becomes something that you can look forward to instead.

One of my favorite things to do is to enjoy dining out, whether it's a new restaurant or one of my favorites. I knew this would be a difficult thing to overcome because it was a favorite pastime of my ex-husband as well. Therefore, I decided that I would create a new normal. I decided that I would go to eat with friends, but if no one was available, I was completely okay with enjoying that time by myself. I don't do it often, but I have come to appreciate it. I also have found an awesome Mexican restaurant where kids eat free on Wednesdays. I take my daughters there at least once a month.

Once I stepped out of that familiar territory of eating with my ex I realized that I can enjoy my own company. I realized that I can do the things that I enjoy even if I do not have someone with me all the time. Now I have even expanded my horizons and gone to the movies alone as well. You will be surprised at what you learn if you just give it a try. Don't think it to be weird to do new things. I believe it is simple to define things as "weird" because as a result of being accustomed to them being a certain way. It's okay to create new things to do and invite change into your life.

Through being open to change, I learned to become okay with who I am outside of the role of being a wife. One strategy that I also started to incorporate during my divorce process was practicing gratitude. Each day I would wake up and list off five things I was grateful for. If ever I felt like there was nothing, which was often, I would remind myself of the things in my life I was overlooking and the things I could not live without. Sometimes we forget to thank God for our health, our homes, heat, food, the finances to be able to pay bills, a car to get us to and fro, and a job, because some people don't have them. Gratitude was important to me because when I would wake up, I would often go into an instant state of depression. Sleep makes it easy to "escape" from everything, but when you're awake you have to face it. I decided that instead of waking up thinking of the things that were going wrong, I would be intentional about focusing on the things that were going right. This gratitude practice encourages me and it gives me a lot of motivation to push towards the future because I remember that there are so many things that I can look forward to instead of focusing on the things that I regret.

Research shows that our life is actually a reflection of our thoughts. If you think about negative things, you're going to notice and internalize negativity every day. If you think of positive things you will have more positivity in your life. Choose to shift your focus mentally and you will notice your world shift as well.

Taking action
"There's an old saying that says doing the same thing over again expecting a different result is the definition of insanity. Don't be insane. Do something different if you truly want something different."
-Dr. Nicolya

I recently bought a new car, and it has some cool features. One feature that excites me is the automatic windshield wipers. For several days after having the car I prayed for rain. After having the car for about a week, there was finally rain in the forecast. That day I had a few errands to run so I knew this would a good time to test out that particular feature. Shortly after my first stop to a doctor's appointment, it began to rain. At first it was sprinkling, so the wipers didn't turn on automatically. This made sense to me because it wasn't pouring. As the rain progressed to a full downpour, the wipers still didn't turn on. I got angry and frustrated and it took me nearly two minutes to manually start the wipers. Before that I had considered pulling over to see if they eventually would turn on because at this point I was thinking it was a manufacturer defect. I reached out to the dealership later that day and found out that I needed to change the setting in order to activate the feature.

After getting off the phone with the dealership, my spirit was heavy in realizing how we often wait in frustration but refuse to take action. We want to be happy again, but won't let go of our victim mentality. We want to move forward, but won't let go of the past. We want to not hurt anymore, but we get too familiar and comfortable in our state of depression. Things won't just happen without intentional action. We can't expect to go through a devastating divorce and then just wake up happy one day. We have to put in the work to heal ourselves. It's the same thing with prayer. You can go to God in prayer as often as you'd like, but you have to meet him there. You can't ask for patience then refuse to practice it when the opportunity arises. You can't ask for healing then refuse to implement a plan to truly heal. Going through a divorce is tough. But if you use that as an excuse to just pull over and sit on the freeway and wait for your "windshield wipers" to come back on, you're not going to get very far.

Choosing to heal is a risk, but one that needs to be taken. We often run from healing because healing hurts. It doesn't feed our ego, but it instead challenges our emotions. I have come to know that healing is the only way to live a full life. Taking no risks will end up being the biggest risk of your entire life. You have to risk failure to find success, you have to risk rejection to find acceptance, you have to risk heartbreak to love, and you have to risk hurting in order to heal. If you're always avoiding risk, you're missing out on life.

You can also work on taking action by being intentional

about your choices. After my divorce I was so broken and bitter. It was exhausting to relive it every single day. The problem was that I did not believe I could break free from the pain. My divorce happened to me and because that did not change, I felt like I would be stuck feeling this way forever. I decided to hire a coach who shared with me that I could find happiness again. The problem was that she believed this, but I didn't. Truthfully, I was impatient so going through a healing process was not anything I was looking forward to. I wanted a magic pill to take the pain away and then I would believe things could get better. We all know there is no quick route to anywhere with going.

So after a lot of push back and some resentment I decided that I would put in the work to heal my hurt. Through these last few years, personal development has been my number one priority and focus. Through this experience of focusing on developing myself and strengthening my resolve I learned that I had been living by default. I allowed what happened to me to be my excuse to stay stuck. I allowed being divorced to take over my life and ultimately control me. My coach was able to show me that living my default is an awful way to live and inspired me to begin living by design. Living by design is an intention way of living where instead of focusing on all of the things going wrong, you chose to put your focus into living a life based on your goals and desires.

Here are some characteristics of living by default:
- **You have no meaningful dreams.** You don't know what you want to achieve in the short term or the long term. Or you may have goals and dreams that others have created for you or that you feel obligated to accomplish.
- **You have no plan on how to reach your dreams.** You may have a dream, but you don't have a plan on how to make it a reality. Therefore, you're making no progress other than simply dreaming.
- **You don't take action according to your plan.** You may have a dream and a plan, but you don't put your plan into action. Maybe it's too much work, or you have convinced yourself that the dream is too BIG or you're not good enough. As a result, nothing happens.
- **You aren't consistent in your effort.** You may have a dream, a plan, and take some action towards it, but your

effort isn't consistent. You often grow impatient with the process and throw in the towel.

If you checked yes to these are allowing your situation and emotions to control your life. What would happen if you started to be more intentional in your approach to life? How would your life change? Make a plan today to start living intentionally.

In order to live more intentionally you first must create a plan. Take some time to consider what is the thing that motivates you and what do you feel like you are on earth to do. Even if you do not know these answers you do know that you were not called to soak in bitterness, depression and anger for the rest of your life. So seek to find these answers. Dig deep. Consider a time you were happy or felt fulfilled. How were you spending your time, who did you have around you, what made you feel the best? Once you identify the answers to these questions foster this plan. You can't a target that isn't defined. In other words, to accomplish your goals they need to be clearly defined. Once you know what you desire to accomplish and seek start creating a plan to make it happen. It is important to proactively plan. Proactive planning includes understanding what changes are necessary in order to reach your next level. Consider a coach to support you on the journey so that you will continue to push yourself and stay motivated.

The next step is to understand that this process takes time, so it is important to take care of yourself. You can't be valuable to the people that count on you without first taking care of yourself. Self-care is so important when going through a painful time. We have to make our emotional, mental and physical health a priority if we are truly determined to get well. Find one activity that you can take part in that will help lift your spirits. It can be something major like taking trips or it can be something smaller, such a mediating daily. The goal is to take care of yourself before you lose yourself.

Take a moment to reflect on where you are. If you are comfortable playing victim to your situation, it's time to break free from that otherwise your divorce will rule and take over your life. You have a choice. You can decide to make changes. You can decide to live again. You can decide to find happiness. You just have to believe that not only with your mind, but with your actions as well. Life is far too short and valuable to go through life waiting and wishing things were happening. Start taking action today.

How do I build resilience?
Life doesn't get easier or more forgiving, we get stronger and more resilient"
- Steve Maraboli

The quickest way to build your resilience muscle is to stop fighting resistance. Allow each obstacle and change life throws your way to be your chance to build your resolve and in turn your resistance. The only thing constant in the world is change so you will need it.

When my youngest daughter began first grade it started off well! She came home daily telling me all of the new things she was learning. As soon as the new beginning wore off she started complaining. After she was able to calm down I asked her, "What's going on, why are you so upset?" My daughter shared with me that she just she didn't like 1st grade. When we got to the bottom of it, she missed her kindergarten teacher who was awesome. She also missed the friends that she had in her first grade class and the extra recess she once had. First grade was a little bit more difficult, but not impossible. She was missing the ease and comfort of it all.

So I explained change to her. While change can feel not so fun, it is often the best thing for us. We talked about how first grade is an opportunity to mature, grow and learn. This conversation and experience with my daughter made me think about us as adults. We often try to avoid change like the plague. How many times does change come in our life and knock us on our butt? We enjoy life when we feel like everything is going well and then BAM this hurdle comes that we just can't seem to jump over no matter how hard we try. In these situations, it's easy to become bitter, or mad and begin to throw an adult version of the tantrum, like my daughter threw. Maybe not falling on the ground kicking and screaming, but we definitely throw internal tantrums. This is where we're giving push back to the change we're not willing to accept it, maybe we're not embracing or trying the new things that go with the change. It happens more than we realize. Imagine you have been working for the same company for 10 years and then you have a new CEO that takes over. This new CEO comes in and changes everything and now you're mad and no longer want to be there to see the change through. Instead of trying to understand the change and truly accepting that change happens, we get angry and resentful and give up.

When you are stepping into unknown territory your body will beg for you to come back to the comfort zone. It seems appealing because it's safe, welcoming and familiar. This is all a lie! A lot of people think a comfort zone is comfortable. NOT TRUE! It's really just familiar, but not at all comfortable. No success happens there no growth happens there. Comfort zones are just what our body associated with comfort because it's truly something that we can relate to because it's familiar to us. Comfort zones aren't any good and that's why change is one of those things that just continuously happens. Change comes to set us free, to mature and grow us, to motivate us. Sometimes that change is bad, sometimes that change is good. Both types of change give us a chance for growth- which is always to our benefit.

Change is the only thing constant in the world. This is a little bit of an oxymoron because change isn't constant but that's the one consistent that we know can happen. You may go through change today, get through it, and then you have another change a year down the road, or 5 years down the road. The point is change can happen at any point if we go through life always being bitter or resentful towards it, we're missing a big chunk of what we're supposed to be learning.

Now I am not saying breaking free of your comfort zone is fun. In fact, change is one of the hardest things to be able to embrace. So I want to share the strategies I use to get through one of the most challenging times in my life. The first step is to acknowledge your fears and then take action around those fears. Ask yourself what it is you're feeling. Is it uncertainty? Is it feelings of insecurity? Is it feelings of being scared? Is it feelings of being overwhelmed? Sadness, anger, all of those feelings are okay and part of the process. What most people misunderstand is that they think that feelings are bad like anger or sadness are bad. It's not anger or sadness that is bad it's what we do with those feelings that can make them healthy or unhealthy.

If you feel angry and journal, listen to music or exercise to feel those endorphins and you start to feel better then that's an appropriate way to handle your anger. If you get rage and you decide that you're going to go flatten your ex's tires that's probably not the best way to handle anger. So understand that feelings alone aren't bad but being able to really process through them is going to be important so the best way to process through those feelings is to just sit and ask yourself, "what is it that I'm feeling" and "why am I feeling this" and journal your way through it. Next start to think of what actions you can take to work through that. Maybe you're worried about becoming the sole provider of your household and that it puts a lot of weight on you.

Sitting in anger and bitterness is not solving it, so if you acknowledge that you feel angry and then create a plan to start looking for another job or extra source of income that is making progress. You may make a plan to update your resume, the next day after that you may decide that you're going to make sure that you have up to date references. After that your goal is to apply for two jobs every single day. Whatever it may be the goal is to create a plan that you can follow through with.

The second step is to stop and ask yourself, "What is it that I should be learning from this?" This is such a critical piece of the healing process. Many people when going through a divorce get so consumed in their pain that they never take time to reflect on what they should be learning from the experience. They spend their time venting, talking and talking about it, but not taking any action to make change. They get on social media and post away, but allow the comments and the sad responses to keep them in the victim mentality. Ultimately if you can truly reflect on what you should be learning from your experience and identify key takeaways then you can truly grow. Not to mention it builds resilience and character. There is a lot of wisdom in our wounds, but if we are so busy covering them up, we will miss it.

Maybe after your divorce you take some time to reflect and you learn that you should never lose so much of yourself in a relationship. Or maybe you decide that you shouldn't rush into a relationship next time. Or you may have learned what role you played in the split, and decide that there are some things you want to work on personally for yourself. Too many people go through life's changes, don't learn anything from it, and then repeat the same choices, and then wonder why they are in the same situations over and over. The definition of insanity is doing the same thing twice expecting a different result. Do something different. Do something drastic. Give yourself a chance to heal.

I am such a big advocate for personal development and when I have bad days I ask myself what I should be learning from that experience. What should I be focused on? I'm constantly looking for ways to develop into a better person and that comes with a lot of reflection and just being willing to grow and develop more into the person that you desire to be. It's not always fun, and it's definitely not easy, but it is always worth it. It takes a lot of work and honesty, but the benefits are amazing.

The final step is event + response = the outcome. The divorce that you went through happened. But your response is what is going to determine the outcome. This makes me think of one of my favorite quotes by Denice Frohman, "The wound is not your fault, but healing is your responsibility". It is our job to react and respond in a way that will help us heal, not keep us stuck hurt or bitter. You see we can't change the divorce, but we can change our reaction and response to it. When going through a divorce it is easy to blame the other person and the situation. When you do this, you let the situation and the other person control your response. It may not always feel like it, but we are in control.

One of the things that I often talk to my clients about is paradigm shifts. Paradigm shifts are simply changing our perspective. This is turning situations around to make them work in your favor. This is choosing to look at our circumstances through an optimistic lens. So, instead of being bitter about your divorce, consider this as a new opportunity to start again. This is an opportunity to find yourself and create a life that you desire. We can't always control the events that change our life, but we can always control our response to it, which in turn controls the outcome.

How to get revenge on your ex
"Nothing makes revenge sweeter than forgiveness and moving on"
- Dr. Nicolya

I know how painful it is to lose your hopes and dreams that were related to your marriage. I know how painful it is to feel let down. I also know how painful it is to be struggling with the hurt of a choice that someone else made that you now have to carry with you. The good news is you can get revenge. Yes, revenge, but not in the same way that you would typically think it should be, like slashing tires, draining bank accounts, exposing your ex, or busting out windows, etc. The best way to get revenge against your ex or anyone else involved is to move on and be happy.

I know that this seems counterintuitive because you're hurt and may want to cause hurt in return. That probably feels like the only way to get even. Maybe this person has stolen things from you, or you're in a financial bind because of the divorce. Perhaps you've lost something in the process of your divorce, or there was infidelity involved, which has caused wounds that are too painful to explain. There could be a myriad of reasons why you want to get revenge on this person, but I am here to tell you that it's not as exciting as you think it would be, and ultimately your response is only going to hurt you. If you're thinking of the best way to get revenge, it needs to be something that is going to work in your favor and not keeping you stuck. If you bust out his windows, that is likely going to result in a police report plus a costly fine or multiple court dates. However, if you're healing, there is no consequence to you.

The best way to get started is to understand the benefit of where you are. This may sound crazy, but there are some good things to consider concerning divorce. One opportunity you get is to redefine who you are. There is a new opportunity to explore independence and what that looks like for you. If you spend your entire post-divorce life looking for revenge, then have you had a chance to redefine and find the best version of yourself? No. You want to use this time to heal and move forward, not stay stuck and in a bitter place focusing on your past. Remember these words: Your future needs you more than your past. If you hold onto your past, you're ultimately missing out on your future.

The first step to get happy and move on is to celebrate that independence. Take some time to ask yourself and reflect on what things look like now that you're single. What does it look like now that you're not sharing decisions or sharing your household? What have you wanted to do that you weren't able to do until now that you're independent? Understand that you can use the negative emotions that have arisen from the ashes as a stepping stone to your happiness. A lot of people assume that once they move on and experience that happiness, that it somehow negates the fact that they were hurt or that they cared about their former mate. Some people also assume that moving forward releases their ex from the pain they caused. When you decide that you're going to move on and be happy, it allows you the opportunity to take what you learned and begin again. It is not excusing their behavior or making light of the painful divorce. It is just permitting you to leave that in the past and move forward to the future you deserve. Holding on to that hurt and pain is not going to get you anywhere; it will only keep you stuck and stagnant. It will not allow you to move on and receive the peace that you desire.

For quite some time, my heart ached because of the way things turned out, but there was an opportunity that presented itself. I had to decide whether I would hold on to the hurt and allow myself to suffer, or acknowledge those emotions and move in the direction of my healing. For a long time, I stayed in that hurt place because it was familiar and felt safe. I know that seems weird, but a lot of us normalize pain and hurt because the alternative is unfamiliar territory. It felt like if I let go and forgave my ex, that it was somehow helping or benefiting him. I learned that forgiveness and moving on is for you. You must let go of what it looks to everyone else and know that ultimately it's for your benefit.

I once had someone share with me that holding onto forgiveness is like drinking poison and expecting the other person to be affected by it. That's exactly what you're doing to your body when you hold on to those negative emotions. You get to pick the direction you desire to go. You have the power in this situation to heal yourself and forgive your ex if you are ready to move in the direction of your future. If you're ready to move on and be happy and get that "revenge" that you deserve, the first step is to celebrate your independence. Embrace the transition.

The next way to get through the desire to get revenge is to create boundaries. Setting boundaries is going to be a significant part of several aspects of the healing process. I remember it being difficult to understand what boundaries would look like during this phase. My entire life revolved around my family, so creating boundaries was a new phenomenon for me. I had to create boundaries around the time that I would answer phone calls from my ex, as well as decide which areas of my life I would continue to allow him to be a part of. I also found it helpful to create boundaries around social media. I had to be careful about what I was posting, who I was friending, and what I was viewing on social media. My friends would say, "I saw your ex out this weekend with a girl" or "Can you believe he shared this on his story??" I thought those were good things for me to know because it prepared me to know that my ex was out dating I could finally let go and be free. What it really did is it kept me stuck, consumed, and worried about what he was doing. It hurt so badly. It kept me in a very dark and depressed state.

Let's consider this example: You set a goal to stay single after you get divorced so you can heal. At some point, you get information via social media that your ex is on a date on what was your former anniversary. As a result of the hurt you feel, you decide to download a dating site because you don't like the idea of them moving on or falling in love before you. You have now disrupted your progress as a result. Boundaries are helpful in this situation because they create a sort of barrier to keep you moving in the direction you're trying to go. Also, avoiding comparison in this situation would be beneficial to your healing process.

While setting boundaries with others is essential, those boundaries won't be effective unless you learn to set healthy boundaries for yourself. You must honor the relationship you have with yourself because it's the longest relationship you will have. You may as well make it worth it. It is imperative to take ownership of all aspects of your life. This includes your thoughts, actions, and words. There are three boundaries you should set for yourself. The first is how you implement self-care. The second is choosing the thoughts that control you. The third is concerning your decision making. While these may be difficult things to share, it is imperative for your growth that you start to implement these boundaries because you're also teaching people how to treat you.

You cannot control your ex; you can only control yourself. A part of that control includes setting those boundaries, creating safe zones, and showing yourself love. Boundaries are the key to your freedom, whether that is being free from those negative emotions or free from feeling stuck.

The next and final step to get revenge is to create goals. Money was always tight when I was married, so investing in my business was never something we could afford to do. As a result, I kept delaying my ideas because it never seemed to be the right time. As soon as I was divorced, I created a vision board of different business ideas. I set a goal and made room for my vision even though it just sounded crazy, and I wasn't yet in a place where I could make the necessary financial investments. I decided to get a part-time job and was able to create a budget to make those investments.

Don't be afraid to set goals. Whether you are seeking financial freedom, a new house, or falling in love again, your goal could be a part of the process of healing the pain that you have carried. Don't overcomplicate the goal setting. It could be as simple as changing a job or your career trajectory. I do recognize that juggling all of the tough emotions, a new life, and trying to set goals can be challenging. One of the best tips to work through this is to get an accountability partner. This may be a coach, a counselor, or a friend.

I hired a coach who helped me to balance in my life. She reminded me of the reasons why it was important to move forward. Once you're able to accomplish something after a considerable loss, it is life-changing. It's incredibly refreshing and reminds you that there are things to look forward to.

A lot of people wear this scarlet letter "S" or "D, representing being separated or divorced. They do this by living with shame and a negative mindset as a result of that failed relationship. They walk around in pain, believing that nothing can change. There's so much that can happen, and so many good things can result if you allow your divorce to be a stepping stone to move into the direction of your dreams. When you go through such a great loss, it can be easy to focus on and be consumed by the negativity. When you have an opportunity to set those goals and work in the direction of them, it changes your whole perspective, and it reminds you that your purpose is more significant than what happened to you.

If I hadn't experienced my divorce, I wouldn't be in a position to support women like you all around the world that are going through the same thing. Because I have been there and lived those difficult emotions, it gives me the ability to support those who need it most. I know what it looks like on the other side I know what it feels like to bounce back, stronger than ever. I know what it's like to feel strengthened, and I know what it's like to feel empowered. I know what it's like to pick yourself up off the floor and go after your dreams. This is why I am so passionate about sharing my truth and the power of healing. I don't want you to be stuck, and I don't want you to be trapped, I don't want you to be bitter or depressed or suicidal or anxious. I want you to be happy. I want you to understand that there is life again after your divorce.

Overcoming Infidelity
Your value doesn't decrease based on someone's inability to see your worth.
~Unknown~

Let's talk about infidelity. I know this is not an ideal topic, a fun topic, or even something you want to discuss during the healing process, but it's important. If you don't confront it, you can't heal it. According to *"Divorce Magazine"* it is estimated that about 45-50% of married women and 50-60% of married men have affairs. Now these numbers can never be truly confirmed, because cheating is not usually something people are willing to admit. According to the American Psychological Association (APA), infidelity in the United States accounted for 20-40 percent of divorces.

This is why I have decided to dedicate an entire chapter to this very topic. I'm realistic in believing that the majority of my clients have faced infidelity or an affair at some point or another. I did as well, and it has taken me years to be able to be open and honest about the impact it has had on my life.

Infidelity can break apart the strongest couples or knock down the strongest people because it is like everything that you thought about your relationship feels like it changed. What we don't realize is when we experience an affair or infidelity in a relationship, we internalize it and conclude that it has to do with us. We allow ourselves to believe thoughts such as "I'm not good enough" or "What did I do wrong". Unfortunately, due to the stigma around infidelity, nobody wants to discuss it. Therefore, you're left feeling alone. I want to take away all the embarrassment and shame and let you know two things; 1: NOTHING is wrong with you and 2: You're not alone.

I was one of those people who did not want to be a single parent. I did not want to be another statistic. I wanted to show my kids something different. As a result, I dug my heels into the relationship, reminding myself I was ALL IN no matter what. When we dated, my ex had multiple affairs, but I wanted to prove my commitment. I wanted to show that I loved him no matter what. With each affair, I dug my heels in even harder clinging to life for my relationship. Although I dug my heels in deeper, I wasn't really forgiving my ex.

I dug my heels in to hold onto the relationship, but never truly discussed it because it hurt so bad. Also, I believed that confronting it was accepting it so I operated like it didn't happen and continued to put on a façade that I was happy. I held on to the belief that each time was his last time cheating. Since the cheating continued to happen it was difficult for me to feel like I could trust him, and in turn I stopped trusting my own judgment. By the time we got married I was so hurt, angry and confused, but continued to dig my heels in because now it was for better or worse.

All in all, that really caused a major breakdown in our marriage. Now when I look back, I realize that the more I dug my heels in, I wasn't showing unconditional love. I was showing that it was okay for me to be treated in a hurtful way. When I think back to that point in my life, I wish that I had known that it was okay to get support, it was okay to go to counseling, and that healing from this is hard work. I could write an entire book on the long term impact that cheating had on my relationship and my self-esteem, but I want to share healing because this is the thing we all need to focus our energy on. I will share a three step strategy that I use with my own clients to start the healing journey.

In order to begin the healing after infidelity you have to confront what happened, what you are feeling and what you have come to believe. I hid from my infidelity for so long because it hurt. From the idea of understanding that it was real, examining myself after it happened, forgiveness and even the idea of having to address it, it all sent me from one extreme to the next. I was either really angry and nasty or I was pretending that nothing ever happened. Sometimes I would believe that if I ignored it, I wouldn't have to face it. The more I pushed it aside, the more those difficult emotions would come back and I knew after some time that they weren't going anywhere. I knew I had to feel it to move past it.

Many people think that in order to confront the affair, you have to do so with your ex. If you're going through the divorce process right now it is probably not a good time to hash out the situation with your ex. To process through it you can consider a counselor, a coach or a journal. You have to reflect on your role in the affair. Not what you did to cause it, because you didn't do anything. It is important to lay out all of the details. even those embarrassing details (i.e. it had been a long time since we had sex, or he asked me to do something I wasn't comfortable doing).

We can't solve what we won't face and this is probably the most difficult part. You're likely wondering how to hash it all out- especially without your ex. The first step is to face it. It is important that you're sensitive with this part of the experience. It is especially important that you take a break if you find yourself wanting justification from your ex. Many people think talking about it with them will help you feel better, but it won't. Many times you open yourself up to the potential of new wounds by sharing that you're healing from pain they have caused. This is why it is important to find a trusted person or a safe space to work through the healing process. You also want to find someone who is not biased or will not judge you through this experience. Take some time today to consider how and when you will be ready to hash out the entire experience and face it head on. Trust and believe that ignoring it and being unforgiving are not helping you get started on the healing process. There is an old saying that goes, "Holding on to unforgiveness is like drinking poison and expecting another person to die." Let it go and work through what you're feeling.

The second step is to understand that affairs or infidelity are not personal. This is huge, and this realization was life changing for me. There are people in this world who have been through everything. Their spouses have been very difficult to deal with or maybe they're is a lack of intimacy in their relationship and they still don't cheat. There are people that have everything including intimacy in their relationship, and they still cheat. Cheating is a personal decision that has nothing to do with anyone else. It doesn't have to do with being tempted by somebody else, it doesn't have to do with a difficult spouse. Cheating is 100% a personal decision.

Here is what we have to understand on the other end of the spectrum: There's nothing that you could have done differently that would have changed the situation. Your spouse made that choice because of something going on within them. When I had I talked it out with my ex-husband prior to our divorce, he shared that with me but I still couldn't accept it. I still wanted to carry the blame because I wanted to create an answer. I wanted to make sense of it. The reality is that you can't make sense of nonsense. When you beat yourself up or take the blame you continue to carry that weight. One thing that I have learned through my entire divorce process is that the choices your ex makes has more to do with them than it can ever have to do with you. When you accept this truth you will be able to begin the healing process.

When you focus on blaming yourself for what your spouse did, you end up trying to heal parts of yourself that wasn't even a problem to begin with. You may have oversexualized yourself to please them, tried to be nicer with your words, be more available or prettier. You are enough just as you are. When you recognize that it had nothing to do with you, you can focus on putting your energy into healing the parts of yourself that need to be healed from the damage that was done.

It's another thing if you're trying to fix yourself to prevent your spouse from cheating, this is not effective because no matter what you fix about yourself, they can still make the decision to cheat. They can find other reasons to be unhappy and you will still feel invalidated or like you're not good enough. When someone cheats it has more to do with parts of themselves that have not been healed than it can ever have to do with you. When you take that same level of energy and you focus on healing the parts of yourself that are hurt then you start to restore your self-love, self-care and confidence that is often drastically impacted after an affair.

When you focus on trying to fix yourself, believing you're the problem you will likely continue to be treated poorly. In turn when you begin to focus on healing yourself and building yourself love you will in turn attract healthier relationships. Remember we teach people how to treat us. If you're constantly believing something is wrong with you and that you're the problem, this will reflect in all of your relationships. When you heal your hurt, stand up for what you believe and set boundaries, you will in turn attract healthier relationships.

In my years of research, working through my own pains associated with infidelity, helping clients and trying to better understand infidelity and cheating, I have learned a lot. There are many reasons for infidelity. Sometimes it is rooted in insecurity. Maybe they didn't feel good enough. This can come from childhood experiences or their own beliefs. Sometimes infidelity happens because of what they have come to believe about relationships or how they have seen others operate in relationships. Sometimes it's an addiction. Sometimes it is a form of power or manipulation. Sadly, there are many different reasons and unfortunately, in most situations we will not get answers. The common denominator is none of these are things can control.

Every day, I talk to people who end up in cycles and multiple relationships with people who continue to cheat. Whether they accept it or not, the reason is because they have normalized cheating. If you're in one relationship and they cheat and you get into another relationship and they cheat and again you get into a third relationship and they cheat, you start to believe that all men cheat or all women cheat. The reality is not everyone is unfaithful in relationships. This is why I stated earlier that we have to put our energy into setting boundaries and healing ourselves so that we set the tone for what we will tolerate in our future relationships. We also have to stop normalizing behavior that is not acceptable.

You are not to blame for any infidelity that may have taken place in your relationship. There is nothing that you can change now, so stop carrying the pressure and guilt like a badge of honor. The choice your ex made was about themselves and not about you. When you can learn to embrace this, it will allow you to begin the healing process.

Getting through the special days while hurting
"You're only in this alone if you choose to be."
-Dr. Nicolya

When it comes to divorce, there's often negative energy that ensues around the holidays such as birthdays, anniversaries, Thanksgiving, Christmas, and Valentine's Day. Pay attention to your emotions during these times. How do you feel about the holiday? Are you scared, sad, depressed, angry, or bitter? Take time to consider why you're feeling these emotions.

A lot of times we struggle with holidays because we have an expectation regarding how they are "supposed" to look. It is imperative to define what the holidays will look like for you when you are newly single. If you enter into the holiday with the mindset that being single is a bad thing or being alone is a negative thing, then you're going to feel negative about everything. If you're walking through the mall and you feel insecure about being alone, you're going to notice every couple. Choose to change your outlook and empower yourself. Own that you're strong enough to be alone in the mall during that particular holiday or to make holiday plans by yourself. This allows you to reframe your thinking around that, and it's a great reminder that nothing is wrong with you.

Another thing that you want to do during this holiday time is to create your plans in advance. The biggest mistake that I see people make during this time is having the understanding that they are struggling with being single, but allowing themselves to stay in that hurt place. Those special dates come up at the same time every single year—plan for them. Do not wait for them to sneak up on you without a plan or may feel sad or find yourself rehashing the things you did in the past on that particular holiday. Plan in advance, especially if you know you will be alone. Take some time to consider who you can connect with during these special moments.

My first Christmas after my divorce was the hardest. I had no clue what to expect. There was an order that our children would split the day with each of us. This order was given five days before Christmas so I did not even have time to try to make last-minute plans. This was my first Christmas waking up all alone. Because I did not know what to expect and I knew other people have done it, I thought that I would be okay. It was devastating for me. It was beyond depressing to wake up and see people posting their families on social media or seeing the tree in my house with all the gifts, but nobody to open them up. It was even more difficult not having anywhere to go.

What I did not know was that the women around me who got

divorced had created plans for themselves so that they were not alone. I thank God that I had a marvelous friend who welcomed me into her house and sat with me. In fact, she made me come to her home because she knew I needed her even though I couldn't express that. When I got to her house we didn't do anything major; however, just her company was beyond helpful. After that day, I took some time to reflect. I regretted not planning my day, but after that experience, I decided that I would never wait for a holiday to happen without having a plan. One thing that I have begun doing with my daughters is volunteering. I have a large family, and several members cook on Thanksgiving morning so we volunteer to serve food to the homeless. Volunteering and serving other people is such a humbling and much-needed experience. I have made that a part of my holiday tradition, which in turn gives me something to look forward to. Sometimes it's tempting to feel sad because you're comparing your life to your friends who are married, have children or may be traveling. The sad reality is that there's an entire population of people who don't have food, are homeless, or don't have family to visit for the holidays. This isn't to diminish your experience, but it does help to give you a better perspective.

When you're planning your holiday, it would be great to consider doing something that you've been putting off for some time. This could be taking a trip that you have wanted to take. There are plenty of travel groups that you could consider joining. Maybe you've been wanting to rearrange your living room. Take time to do it during the holiday season. This can help to give you something to look forward to and an outcome that is also just as exciting. I spent my most recent Thanksgiving break starting the outline for this book. While this does not sound like fun to some, I saw the long term benefit of it, and I was so excited to get started. The point is you can still find fun things to look forward to during this time of year that fit your desires. It does not have to be what society says should be done. After all, you deserve to enjoy the holidays as much as anyone else.

A few years ago, on my birthday, after my divorce I was bitter that nobody would celebrate my birthday for or with me. I had gotten accustomed to my ex-husband and I planning something when we were together, even though I did most of the planning it just felt better to have someone to celebrate with. As each holiday passed, I would get sad because I wanted someone to celebrate with me. After almost two years, I decided that I was not going to sit and sulk any longer. I made the decision that I was going to celebrate my birthday and celebrate me. I decided I would not wait for anyone else to do it. I planned a solo trip to Miami, Florida. I aligned it with a conference I was interested in but made sure to find some "me time" as well. It was such a great experience. I got a chance to meet and befriend some amazing and like-minded women. Two of which have become great friends to this very day. I also had the opportunity to try several new restaurants and went sightseeing. This experience was so freeing to me.

When you're single and going through a divorce days of celebration can be very lonely and you may deal with a lot of isolation. Everyone is celebrating with their loved ones and you feel like you have no one to celebrate with. It reinforced the loneliness that you feel all year long. Times of celebration are also times where the questions pop up. The holiday season is often the time of year when people begin asking about your family and what's going on in your life. This is another reason why you need to have a plan for the holidays. You need to be prepared for these tough questions. That does not mean that you necessarily have to answer the questions, but you should be prepared for the fact that people will feel weird that you don't. And that's okay. I asked my mom to let my family know, in advance of the holiday gatherings, that I was not ready to answer any questions along those lines. Maybe you're a little more confident than I was at that time, and you feel confident enough to be direct about not answering those questions. At any rate, having a plan will help you because you won't be blindsided. Setting that tone and making a plan in advance will help take away some of the overwhelm and stress.

Take care of yourself during this time. Acknowledge what you're feeling and that it's challenging to get through this time. That doesn't mean it's impossible, and that doesn't mean anything is wrong with you. It's just a process, and the good news is the longer you do it, the easier it becomes, or the more you become used to it.

While some family members can be offensive, do not discount the importance of people that are really in your corner during this time. Sometimes people don't know how to support you because they have never been through something as drastic as a divorce or separation. One of the things that I found to be particularly helpful for me was explaining what I needed. You could simply let your family know that you will stop by during dinner, but not stay the entire night. You could ask the family to come to your home because you need extra quality time. Whatever it is, do not be afraid to speak up and share with those that you love. Setting the tone and asking for help and support opens you up and allows you to be able to receive that.

I had a good friend of mine that had a rocky relationship with her family. For a long time in her adult life, she felt alone. After her divorce, it heightened some of the emotions she had already been dealing with. She learned that having reliable friends and a good support network would be the very thing that would get her through a tough time. Her friends, in turn, became her family. In other words, she had to redefine family, but it worked for her.

I strongly suggest avoiding social media temporarily. Engaging in social media is probably one of the hardest things to do during this time. When you log in, you will see everyone feeling happy and having fun, and this can trigger a lot of emotions. Especially if you're alone during the holiday season and everyone seems to be with their family. Consider refraining from social media for a few days before and after the holiday. By the time you log in, the hype will have declined, and people will likely be talking about something different. Do understand that I am not telling you to avoid it because you are not happy for your loved ones and friends. I suggest avoiding it because it can cause you to question your value. It may make you second guess if there is something wrong with you, and that's why you're alone. You are valuable. Do not ever allow social media to make you question this.

Pulling back from social media allowed me a chance to spend some time and focus on me. It allowed me to process where I was in the healing journey and helped me to redefine plans that I wanted to implement moving forward. It prevented me from comparing my life and myself to everyone else's highlight reels. This is why avoiding social media is vital so that you're not getting stuck in that comparison trap or belittling your pain or growth. Take a moment to consider what you will need during the holidays to take care of yourself and to ensure the holidays do not take you out.

How to talk to your children about divorce
"Sometimes divorce is the best thing that can happen to a marriage."
-Bangambiki Habyarimana

Children go through various stages of development and, therefore, will understand and conceptualize divorce differently. When you're talking to them about divorce, it is essential first and foremost that you tailor your discussions to your children based on their maturity.

When I went through my divorce process, both of my daughters blamed themselves, although it had nothing to do with them. One thing that I regularly did with my children before bed was tell them, "No matter what, Mommy loves you." This was a simple and concise statement, but it was my way to reassure them that they couldn't do anything that would change my love for them. They couldn't think of anything that would take my love away. No matter the age of your children, they're going to need repeated reassurances that the divorce is not their fault and that you love them.

The best thing for children, at any age, during this time is routine and consistency. As an educator, I understand that children thrive off of consistency and routine, but especially when a significant change like a divorce happens. Divorce has a way of making everything seem like it is spinning out of control. Children desire to make sense of the divorce and all of the changes. The last thing they need to be is weighed down trying to make sense of less important things. If you always did Saturdays at Grandma's, continue to do so if possible. If Wednesday was family pizza night continue to make that happen. This is a subtle reminder for kids that says life is still familiar and safe.

For all children, your method should be clear and straightforward. It shouldn't include any of the messy details like the last time you and dad were intimate or who had an affair, etc. When you share all of the particulars, children feel like they can fix the problem or that maybe even they're the cause of the divorce. It also puts the pressure on them to try to understand it or handle it. A simple way to share the news would be to say something like, "Daddy and I have decided that we can no longer live together.

This was not an easy decision, but it was a decision that we both agreed to. It has nothing to do with you at all, and we love you still so much." When you're having conversations with your children, it may be helpful to say there will be two homes. Reassure them that they will have an opportunity to see both parents. The best thing you can do is pay attention to their emotional reaction, their responses, and, more importantly, the things they don't say.

Understand that children may have mixed reactions to you sharing this. My youngest daughter responded with a nonchalant attitude. While my oldest daughter was extremely emotional. After some time, they traded places emotionally. My younger daughter started becoming angrier about the divorce, and my older daughter had a passive attitude regarding it. There were periods through the divorce process where they had different emotions. Regardless of how they were displaying their reactions to the divorce, I do believe that they were both hurting, even if it didn't appear that way. That's why it's important to keep things consistent and have conversations with them regularly. If you notice a change in their behavior or their demeanor, inquire and give them the space to express themselves. They will need support during this time.

For younger children, typically ages one through five, parents are tempted not to tell them. They may not tell them because they want to shelter and protect them. Sometimes they think it doesn't matter. While it is especially difficult for all children, young children can't conceptualize it. With their limited cognitive ability, children can develop inaccurate ideas about the cause and effect of divorce. Your job is to watch for the signs of distress, which would include emotional irritability, clinginess, whininess, etc. Be sure to share that this is an adult decision and again reassure that you love them very much. Providing consistent care and nurturing during this time gives children a sense of stability and reassurance.

For middle-aged children, ages 6-11, they have more of an ability to talk about their feelings. Unfortunately, divorce is still a complex subject, so they have a limited understanding of what is truly happening or what role they play in it. For this age, it is important to also watch for signs of distress like fear, anxiety, anger, and sadness. This is often the age where children begin to fantasize about their parents being back together.

With children this age, routine and consistency will be necessary. This provides the familiarity and stability they crave. Although they can talk about their feelings in a better way, it may be helpful to approach the conversation in a creative indirect way. It will feel less threatening. For example, instead of saying, "You seem so mad lately, are you upset about the divorce?" You could say, "Some children have sad feelings during their parent's divorce..." and see how they respond. Books about divorce at this age are also beneficial to give them insight into what they are feeling or what to expect.

For teenagers, they too will often have feelings of anger, sadness, irritability, and also sometimes rebellion. The trouble with teens is they are often going through puberty, so it can be challenging to know if their emotions are in response to the divorce or their hormones. When you're having a conversation about divorce, you have to understand that teenagers are a little bit more observant than we'd like to admit. The best thing that you can do as a parent of a teen is have open, calm conversation. Support your teenager's emotional reactions and continue to maintain a high expectation for their behavior. I can't tell you how many parents feel guilty because of their divorce, and they allow their teenagers to get away with different behaviors and choices. I understand the guilt feeling, but that's no excuse for allowing poor behavior because it's ultimately not teaching them anything. In turn, it is only harming them. When you hold them to the high expectations for their behavior and ask them to maintain it, it's teaching them to build resilience, which says that regardless of what happens to them, they can still pick up the pieces. We as adults still need to be able to go to work, raise children, and pay the bills despite what is going on personally, so you're teaching your children a necessary life skill.

Also, for older children, divorce may not come as a surprise. Maybe they've had people in their life that have experienced a divorce. Perhaps they heard you arguing, so they expected this conversation. For younger children, it still may be a shock. Regardless, both age groups are going to have questions that they're afraid to ask. You can end the conversation with, "I understand that this is a lot of information, so if you have questions later, you're always welcome to come and ask me." Ultimately, questions may evolve. It's important to give your children repeated opportunities to ask questions, so continually reinforce this idea that they can ask questions.

When I'm talking to parents, this is one of the biggest mistakes I see. They have one conversation and check it off the list. Talking about divorce is not a one and done type of conversation. Unfortunately, many parents don't allow their children to ask questions and also fail to acknowledge the impact of the divorce. Some parents believe that it's between adults and they never talk about it with their children at all. Ultimately, it changes their life as much as it changes ours, if not more. Our children also notice the emotional responses of both parents; this is why an open line of communication is critical. Otherwise, they likely have a lot of thoughts and emotions stirring around and nothing to do with them.

The focus of children, when they find out about the divorce, is typically on whether they will be secure and safe because ultimately, that's what they need. They will likely wonder how divorce will change their life. They expect it to change their life, but maybe they don't know the extent. This is why it's important to make these things clear. Let them know how things may change, and what things will remain the same. You could even consider helping them to brainstorm how they will talk to their friends about it.

The following are some questions that children may have that you can find a way to add into your conversation: Is it my fault? Is there anything that I could have done to make it better? Is there anything I can do to make it better now? If I behave or if I change certain patterns and behaviors will you guys get back together? Do you guys not love me anymore? How often will I get to see each of you? Will I get to talk to you? How will our family change? Will I have to change schools or change houses? Will we have enough money to live? Be sure to consider these questions, so when they come, you have the answers. Or, consider these questions so that you naturally answer them within your talk. I can't say this enough: Reinforce the idea that they were not responsible for it at all.

The keys to answering these questions are clarity, honesty, and reassurance. Be upfront with the answers, but again, don't involve them in the messy details. Talking to your children is probably one of the most challenging steps, but it's one of the most important steps that you can do to have them farewell after a divorce

I spent several months beating myself up because I never talked to my children about the divorce. What I came to learn was that it is never too late to talk to them. After a few months, I was able to have a conversation and find ways in which I could provide support for them during the divorce. You can never talk to them too late, and you can never open the door for communication too much. I share this to let you know that divorcing isn't easy, and yes, you will have bumps along the road. You won't handle everything correctly, and that is part of the process. But you only fail if you remain on the ground. Get back up, dust yourself off, reflect on what needs to be changed and move forward with success.

How to co-parent effectively
"This is probably one of the most difficult challenges any parent could face - learning to love the other parent enough to make the children first."
-Iyanla Vanzant

Research shows that three main factors that help children to have a better post-life adjustment. The first is having a strong relationship with both parents, the second, having good parenting on both sides, and the third is having minimal exposure to conflict. None of these factors are surprising, but the trouble is how do you pull it off as parents? The best way to make it happen is through co-parenting. Co-parenting is coming together as a team for your children in order to raise your children successfully despite being apart. What I want you to understand is that co-parenting is not a competition. It is collaborating with the best interest of your children in mind. It's working to create a lifestyle that works for your children, not against them. While co-parenting is challenging for most couples, it doesn't have to be impossible. The reason that co-parenting is challenging is that they're no longer on the same page, and co-parenting makes that even more complicated. If you guys aren't on the same page, you also don't live together, but you're trying to raise children together, that can be extremely overwhelming.

Each co-parenting relationship looks different, and ultimately you will need to do what works best for both parties. I do have some suggestions that I have seen work, with both myself and with my clients. Do note that co-parenting effectively is the goal, and sometimes on the way to that goal, you may have to refine it a little bit. Just because it isn't a piece of cake or just because it doesn't work each time perfectly does not mean that you're doing something wrong. It just takes practice and, more importantly, time. I could write an entire book on co-parenting, but I did want to include a brief overview here. Understand that while co-parenting is the best thing for children, I am aware that this is not something that every family can do. These tips are not to make you feel guilty. All you can do is your best and know that children see that, and that is what matters most.

Before co-parenting can work, both parties need to focus on healing. If either person is holding on to anger, resentment or hurt from the former marriage or relationship, they're going to bring that into their co-parenting relationship. It's more tempting to take things personally in a co-parenting relationship when you're dealing with the hurt and unforgiveness from the previous relationship. Healing is going to be a key factor. The trouble is that each person heals in their own time and in their own unique way.

If you desire to heal, know that this is going to include support such as hiring a coach, seeing a counselor, or joining a support group. These are great ways to get you started when on your healing journey. More importantly, they help you see things about yourself that you may not notice on your own accord. This important not only for the co-parenting relationship, but for your continued growth as you move forward as an individual. Having this support will help you to go into the next chapter of your life with success.

  The difficult part is that you can only make the decision for yourself you cannot force your ex to heal. Therefore, if your ex is not ready for healing, your job is to make sure that you have taken steps to heal. Lead by example for both your children as well as your ex. While you can't control your ex, your healing will be a positive visual for your ex to see what could be possible with healing. It also ensures that you're less likely to be pulled into toxic arguments because you're less likely to move on emotion when you're healed. In addition, you're teaching your children through your actions as well. So set an example that is admirable.

  With co-parenting, you must understand that you two will not always see eye to eye. It's unrealistic in a marriage, but especially true with co-parenting. Through co-parenting relationships; disagreements will arise; the best thing that you can do is to keep the disagreements, especially the hostile ones away from the children. Children need to see that their parents are working together for their good and not constantly arguing. Otherwise that reinforces the idea and the thoughts that the divorce is their responsibility and their fault. This is often what many children think. If you notice that you all are having a disagreement, you can ask for a moment to regroup, rethink, and talk later. When you take time to pull away from it, you're able to go in level-headed, less emotional, and have a normal conversation. As a result, the communication has the potential to improve.

  An essential strategy in the co-parenting relationship is flexibility. This can be challenging especially if you didn't have to do a lot of this in a marriage. As a couple, you likely had routines for different holidays. You may have spent one holiday with your family and another with his. Or maybe you split the day. Whatever the routine was, you typically had a plan for these special days. With divorce, this often throws a wrench in your routines. This can be challenging because so many things are already changing in your life and everyone wants a sense of normalcy.

The best thing that you can do in this situation is to be flexible. When you're flexible, you're more likely to receive that in return. Also, being flexible shows your children that you two are working together. For example, although you may be scheduled to have the kids on Thanksgiving, you could show flexibility by allowing the children to spend the Thanksgiving holiday with your co-parent because you know that he has family in town that the children don't often get to see. Or, maybe there's a weekend where your ex has to swap due to their work schedule. If you're available don't throw up their poor planning, but step into help with your children graciously. You never know when you may need something similar in return.

Whatever comes up, try to be as flexible as possible. Obviously, you want to keep the consistency in the routine, but if you can be flexible when the time is needed, you're really setting a positive example for your children and also reducing the likelihood of conflicts. If you know that there's a special day or something important to your ex, try to have your children participate in it, even if it's not something that you're excited about. For example, if you know that your ex's birthday is coming up, have your children make a card. This is a great way to show your children that it's okay to love their father or their mother, and it's a great way to show your ex that even though you guys are separated that you haven't separated them from your children's life.

The next step is to be accessible to your co-parent. Now this is not without boundaries where they can text or call or email any hour of the day, and you're responding right away. Being accessible means not allowing anger or frustration to prevent you from communicating in a timely manner. Failing to communicate will often trigger bigger issues, so if you know that there's something that you can respond to, respond. This keeps the arguments, confusion and the confrontations down as well. It also reduces the likelihood of miscommunication.

Another component to co-parenting effectively is never to badmouth your ex. Obviously, there will be moments where you think of things that you want to share, or your children share things that were said about you. Never stoop to the level where you need to badmouth your ex. Always take the high road, and it'll benefit you in the long run. When you badmouth your ex, you continue the practice of entertaining negative thoughts, which manifest in the way you feel and respond. This is never a good example for your children.

Co-parenting is a big adjustment, but it's something you're likely in for the long haul. The best piece of advice that I can share with you through this process is to choose your battles wisely. If you are always looking for reasons to confront, negate or belittle your ex or if they are doing the same to you the co-parenting relationship with exhaust you and wear you down. So choose what battles are worth fighting for. If your daughter comes home without socks that may not be worth calling and getting all up in arms about. You want to save your energy for the things that are truly important or most pressing matters. When you get offended, or argue about every little eventually your voice won't even be heard. If you feel the need to vent or process call a trusted friend, but everything doesn't need to turn into a big argument. One strategy I would use, as not to exhaust my friends or share all of my business is I would write out a "text" in my phone using my notes app and then not send it. It allowed me to process my frustration without it turning into a major argument.

When co-parenting effectively, it is vital to make adult decisions with adults only. It is also important that you process frustrating situations with trusted adults not your children. As a single parent, it can be tempting to include your children in decisions because they are there or maybe you think they are mature enough to handle it. Kids should never be put in the middle between parents. It is a terrible place for them to be and extremely inappropriate. Included with this, be sure not to share stories of what went wrong in your marriage with your children. Many parents do this so their children aren't upset with them or to give a better "understanding" of why mommy and daddy aren't together anymore.

While it seems like it is helping them process you have to be careful how you share this information. My client shared with her daughter that her father was abusive and that is why she left him. While she believed she was protecting her daughter her daughter came to believe that it was genetic and something was wrong with her too. The daughter also came to resent the mother for some time since she still had to go there. Sometimes children can misinterpret what you're sharing or may even assume that they are at fault. There is a time that it becomes appropriate to talk to children, but when you do it from a place of anger, fear or in midst of a separation or divorce it's difficult to be rational.

Ultimately, no matter what happened in your marriage or how

frustrated you are with your ex, your children still love them, and it's still a part of who they are. Therefore, if you have an adult conversation or an adult decision, talk to another adult. If it's a decision that directly includes your ex, talk to your ex. I know that it's tempting to include friends and family members in those decisions, but this often can make things worse as you may get bad advice, or it may cause more confusion or frustration. The co-parenting relationship is between you and your ex. Bringing other people into that relationship is not always healthy. If you and your ex have a contentious relationship this is when you have to make a judgment call, but it should still not include children.

To be honest, co-parenting is extremely challenging. You could follow every step and still find some struggles with it. There are moments where it works well, and then there are moments where it's a huge challenge. Be patient with yourself through the process. Your job is to do the best you can in that relationship. Take some time to reflect on the strategies you have used and whether they have helped. If they did keep going at it. Cheers to you! If they did not, regroup and think about what changes you can make on your part. The reality is co-parenting goes beyond your children's 18th birthday or high school graduation. You will see each other at important events for your children, future grandchildren, etc. You have to learn to look at the relationship in a positive way and make the most of it while you can.

Remember while co-parenting is between your ex and yourself, you can only control your role in the relationship. When you're able to keep that in mind and focus on your part you won't become bitter or exhausted trying to control things that are not within your control. Keep your children in your mind and remember your words, actions, and choices are setting an example for them. It can be positive or negative, you get to decide. Don't be so consumed in what part your ex isn't taking care of what they may be saying about you or even their behavior. Children are resilient, and they are also attentive. You stay the course. Stay encouraged. It won't be difficult forever, even if it feels that way.

How to handle bad mouthing
"What other people say about you is their reality, not yours."
-Unknown

Going through a divorce is already one of the most challenging things that you can go through. So, what happens when your ex hits below the belt? Maybe they bashed you on social media or badmouthed you to another person. What happens if it's pervasive? This happens to many people who are going through a divorce so I want to let you know that you're not alone.

The majority of divorced couples occasionally say something less than kind about their former spouse. This doesn't make it okay, but it's a part of the healing process. When your ex bashes you, whether publicly or privately, to a friend or your children, it's proof that the person is hurt. They could be trying to heal, and there's pain that they're trying to process, or they could be trying to cover up their pain with bad mouthing. In reality, we don't say bad things about people or situations we don't care about. The fact that they're still bashing you or looking for reasons to talk about you shows that there are still feelings that need to heal.

The best response is no response. You don't have to feel the need to defend yourself. That's ultimately what the person wants. They want a reaction, and when you try to defend yourself, you end up looking as foolish as they do. In Jay-Z's song Takeover he says: "Never argue with fools because from a distance, people don't know who's who." This is so true. When two people are arguing, they both end up looking like fools no matter who began the argument and no matter who is right. Imagine a random person on social media and all they see is your ex talking bad about you. Next, they see you talk about your ex, and they're in the middle trying to piece together the story that they shouldn't even be involved in. This happens all the time. It is especially true for mutual friends who hear both sides. Eventually it becomes awkward and people assume that both sides have just lost their cool.

It's difficult to remain calm or quiet when this is happening. We have this desire to defend ourselves because it seems like the right thing to do, but I cannot tell you how many times people that take the higher road end up faring well. People don't have to go on their social media page's and wonder what's going on. People don't have access to parts of your life that should be private. When you respond, you're engaging and entertaining the drama. When you don't respond, it eventually becomes incredibly boring for your ex to continue to attack you. Think about it like this: if you were upset, would you argue with a wall? Probably not, because there is no reaction, no engagement and ultimately no point. The same goes for your ex. If they're upset with you and they're saying hurtful things to get a reaction, and you don't argue with them, eventually they understand that their behavior and their statements have no impact on you.

If your ex badmouths you and you feel the temptation to defend it, do something different instead. Find a trusted close friend or family member that you can vent to, that you can share what you're feeling. You can also use this time and consider journaling. But do not let your ex know that it's getting under your skin. I used to write a note "to my ex," but really, the note was to myself. When I was done writing, I felt calmer, and then the last little bit of frustration I did have, I would use that to tear the paper. It was a good release for me. I did not have to feel the pressure of carrying around those heavy emotions any longer. It also was a safe and objective way to release some of the tension and stress.

When your ex badmouths you the next step is to avoid matching your ex's intensity. Imagine having your ex as a toddler throwing a tantrum. Think about it like that. They're just a toddler. What's the best way that you would handle the situation? Would you respond by getting on the floor and kicking and screaming and throwing your own tantrum, too? Or do you remain calm and set limits? Ultimately no parent will get on the floor and throw tantrums with their children. This also proves my point. It's never a good idea to mimic childlike behavior with your ex because, ultimately, it doesn't solve it. When they are sending nasty messages, remember you get to choose whether you engage. You do not have a responsibility to respond to every hostile text, email, or comment that they make. Choosing to avoid confrontation is also prioritizing peace.

There are some situations where you may feel the need to confront the badmouthing. For example, maybe they've shared something with your student's school or your children's doctor, etc. Whatever you do, don't counter-attack at your ex. Meaning, don't launch into an emotional, frustrated state explaining why your ex is the crazy one. Present your side calmly and factually. Ultimately people are going to believe what they want to believe. Your job is to be the bigger person and to allow your actions to speak for you. From my perspective, as well as being an educator and a coach, I have seen many custody battles gone wrong. The parent who was able to respond calmly and have a sensible conversation, backing it up with facts or paperwork, was in a position to be listened to and supported.

Do not allow yourself to get emotional. It's natural to feel angry and upset, especially when people say bad things about you. However, if you come across as emotional or volatile, others will begin to believe those things. You cannot control what other people heard, but you can control your behavior so that they can develop their own thoughts regarding it. Remember that your ex's comments and his beliefs have nothing to do with you or with your worth. They don't say whether you're a bad person or a good person. Only you know that.

Take comfort in knowing that if your ex has taken time to bad mouth you to your children, that they will eventually figure things out. Children pay attention to patterns of behavior and usually can make accurate judgments of situations, although it will take time. Do not repeat the situation to your children. Allow it to fizzle out as they express it. Say, "Thank you for that information." If it's something that you can correct calmly, do so and then move forward. For example, maybe your ex isn't being truthful about the attempts to be involved in their life, and he tells the children something indicating that you are not allowing him to be involved in extra-curricular activities for the children. The reality is that your ex should already know about their activities based on them being enrolled in the school system or him having access to a shared calendar.

In response to your children saying "Mom, why didn't you tell dad about my concert? Why won't you let him be around anymore?" You could say, "Wow, that's a really great question. I would love for your dad to be around. Unfortunately, I don't know if dad forgot to put it on his calendar." This puts the responsibility back onto the other parent without you badmouthing him. That's an easy way to address it without putting yourself at fault, and also without it being an emotional response.

During the process of my divorce, my ex and I would do the pickup and drop off exchange with our children about 15 minutes from my home. While to some, this drive may seem annoying, I actually liked it. Every time my children would get in the car at the end of a visit, they would share different things that were said about me at their father's house. Since they were in the backseat, I had a good chance to calm my facial expressions, take a minute to think, and then respond. Sometimes I would even say, "Well, I'm not sure what to say to that, give me a moment," and I would take a minute to regroup. I was responding from a calm and secure place and not from a place of frustration, anger, bitterness or hurt.

At the end of the day, when you're being talked about, know this truth: The people in your life who matter don't mind. The people who mind, don't matter. This means the people who love you and care about you and are meant to be in your life will not care what is said. The people who are listening to the badmouthing about you, do not matter. Remember that the information, the bad mouthing and the things that your ex is saying or sharing about you, whether publicly or privately, is not your fault and it's not personal. Hurt people hurt people. Your job is to focus on your healing.

Getting help legally
"Rock Bottom became the solid foundation on which I rebuilt my life."
-J.K. Rowling

If you're contemplating or beginning a divorce, you may be overwhelmed with the amount of information available to you on the internet, especially concerning the legal matters. The truth is there is no perfect answer or approach because every divorce is so unique. Some people go through dissolutions and can agree on everything and are done within weeks, while other people can't agree on one thing and spend $50,000 on divorce fees and lawyers and are fighting in court for years. Most people fall somewhere in between.

Although divorce is one of the most complex and emotional legal processes, not every couple needs court assistance to end their marriage. If you and your spouse are on the same page about what you want for your family, you may be able to negotiate a divorce settlement on your own. This is ultimately the best route to take. Unfortunately, this is not always the case.

Divorce can be complicated, emotionally draining, and life-changing. Hiring a divorce lawyer doesn't need to add to that complication. If you do your research and interview prospective lawyers well enough, you can choose a lawyer who best suits your needs and can get you through the process as smoothly as possible. You may even consider asking around for referrals.

First, you should decide whether or not you need an attorney. Maybe you and your ex don't have a ton of assets, and you don't have children. In this case, it can be easier to settle and agree to work together. Maybe the two of you just decided that you can come up with a settlement that works for both parties. If you're on the other end and your spouse is abusive or controlling, or you two have a lot of marital assets, and you have children, or you two can't agree, then it will be in your best interest to hire an attorney.

The next step is to research your area. Check the reviews on the law firm, and check their website. Consider what kind of cases they have helped with, and review their pricing. Also, you can ask family and friends for recommendations. Even if they don't know family law attorneys, they may know other attorneys who could provide professional guidance. Some attorneys will only work with specific genders only, so pay attention to that as well. Look for general information about divorce or family law, or blog posts about developments in family law. High-quality attorneys will stay informed in their area of law and have an interest in educating their clients and website visitors. Look for years of experience and their area of expertise.

While cost may seem important, you will ultimately get what you pay for. Do not make finding the cheapest lawyer your focus. This is not a decision to be settled lightly. Some attorneys will charge you a simple flat rate for a divorce, while others will bill you by the hour. The more complicated your divorce, the less likely you'll be offered a flat rate, and the more expensive it will be. Take this into consideration. I know that cost is a sensitive topic, but when battling in court, it is important to put it in the hands of people who truly know the law. If you are low income or on a fixed income, there are options for you. You can contact a legal aid society, find an independent pro bono lawyer, or you can arrange a payment plan that works for your budget with the lawyer you hire.

After you have identified a few lawyers that you're considering hiring, you will want to go to your state-specific bar association and look up each attorney on your list. You want to make sure that they don't have an excessive amount of formal complaints or any disciplinary action against them. For example, if an attorney has had complaints from former clients, this could be a red flag. This indicates that you may experience issues consistent with the complaints that have been filed.

This is good information to consider. Remember, just because all attorneys took the bar, does not mean they are all equally as qualified. Most lawyers will consult for free, so I recommend taking advantage of the free consultation and get a feel for the attorney you may consider hiring. I had three consultations before finalizing the attorney I decided to work with. When you have these consultations, come prepared with questions regarding their practice, their expertise, but also your case. You want to know for sure they understand case-specific details and are comfortable supporting you with it. (i.e. child custody or domestic violence).

Now, this may go against popular belief, but you want to hire a confident attorney because, in court battles, it is literally your attorney against the other. You need an attorney that can match the demeanor of your ex's attorney. Pay attention to how the attorney interacts with staff members. Watch how staff members approach the attorney and whether their relationship seems more cooperative or authoritarian. When you're asking questions, take note not only of what the lawyer's answer is, but how he/she responds to you. Is the attorney annoyed with your query, or is he/she belittling you? Is she open and engaged or hostile and dismissive? You're going to have a lot of questions throughout the process, so you want someone who can answer them honestly and is patient with you.

Finally, after you consult with a few attorneys, take time to weigh out the pros and cons of each. You will need to make a BIG decision and it can't be done on emotion or in haste. Don't just hire someone because they are the cheapest, especially if they can't confidently answer your questions. If at any time during an interview, you felt uncomfortable or ill at ease with an attorney, that's a red flag that you shouldn't hire him/her regardless of any recommendations from others. This is your case and this is your life. You have to make decisions that will help you to fare well in the long run. Finally, when you make your choice, pray about it for confirmation. When received let the attorney know that you desire to work with them. Schedule the next session so that you can layout the next steps. I know this sounds cliché, but one thing that kept me encouraged in court was not my attorney, but I felt encouraged because I knew God was ultimately going to battle for me. There were so many times God showed up and showed out for my case even when it looked bleak. Know that God will fight your battles too (Exodus 14:14). Stay encouraged.

Forgiveness

"It's one of the greatest gifts you can give yourself to forgive.
Forgive everybody"
-Maya Angelou

Some of the lyrics to my favorite gospel song 'Tis so sweet to trust in Jesus are, "Oh, for grace to trust Him more…". I remember singing this during the time I was trying to break free of the hold that my failed marriage had on me. I was literally thinking and dreaming about it all day. I felt so unworthy and so unlovable. I remember carrying this weight and being embarrassed and feeling ashamed, not feeling good enough and I wanted to be able to trust God more. I remember going into prayer and reminding God of his word. It says that everything works together for our good. I just didn't understand and would ask why this was happening to me. I remember during this time of prayer, I felt this continuous tugging on my heart for forgiveness. I thought I was already forgiving my ex, but if I am honest with myself I wasn't. I hadn't truly forgiven because I did not want to let him "off the hook". I hadn't forgiven because I thought that meant I was accepting his choices. I realized that I wasn't effective in forgiving him because truthfully it was too hard.

Forgiveness is defined as a conscious and deliberate decision to release feelings of resentment and anger towards another who has offended or harmed you. When you look at it like that and when you're faced with the choice, forgiveness is hard. We all know it's easy to forgive people that are sorry, but what about those who never say sorry? What about the ones who say sorry but keep doing the same thing? Where God really calls us to forgive is when it's difficult. True forgiveness occurs when you forgive those who don't really deserve it. This is also a sign of trusting in God. In turn, if you don't forgive, you are going to continue to carry their weight. Now, I know many of you are in this situation and not only did your spouse cheat, but maybe they moved out and they're living with the person they cheated with. Maybe your spouse cheated and is broadcasting it on social media, and you feel embarrassed. Maybe your spouse cheated and had a child as a result, and this was extremely painful. There's a lot of reasons and justification for why you shouldn't forgive, but we have to choose forgiveness anyways.

I want to highlight an important aspect of forgiveness-it is not the same as acceptance. Forgiveness is not saying, "I like what you did." Forgiveness is simply saying that I choose to move forward despite what you did. Forgiveness is saying, "I changed to focus on healing despite what you did. I choose to take care of me despite what happened to me. I choose to heal despite what hurt me." Forgiveness is by far the most important in the most pivotal step in this entire divorce healing process. Do not skip it.

Forgiveness is for you, not for them. You're not doing them a favor to forgive, you're helping yourself. Every night I would go to sleep angry and in real pain. I remember several nights laying down with my hand on my chest feeling physical pain. It was awful. I would think about all the bad things that happened in our relationship. I would stay up late with anger in my heart and anxiety crippling me. These thoughts were keeping me up every single night. I was losing so much weight that people were beginning to wonder if I ate at all. I cried multiple times a day, dealt with sadness and even rage. I was an emotional rollercoaster and I was exhausted. The reality though, is that my ex was not impacted one bit. He went to sleep peacefully each night and woke up well rested the next. I remember seeing him out one time and he was actually happy. I was miserable. In that moment that is when I realized that my unforgiveness had punished me, NOT him.

That is when I knew I needed to really practice forgiveness the way God calls us too. This might have been the most difficult part of the journey, but just like I tell my clients I will tell you. You will NOT make progress in healing without forgiveness. So my journey began. I prayed to see him more as a human that makes mistakes, and not as this terrible person. Every day when I would look in the mirror and say my affirmations, afterward I would follow up and say "I choose to forgive him today, I choose to forgive him today."

Sometimes I would have to take it a step further and remind myself why I was choosing to forgive him, because trust me most days I did not want to forgive at all. I would say "I choose to forgive him today because I desire peace." or "I choose to forgive him today because this is my children's father and I need to love him to let them know they can love him." or "I choose to forgive him today so that I can see him in the same way that God sees him." Some other examples you can use are: "I choose to forgive him today because it's necessary for my healing." or "I choose to forgive him today because I want to love again."

Forgiveness is not a choice, and it is one you have to make daily. It's not a one and done. There are going to be days you don't feel like it, and there will also be days when it's easier. On both days chose forgiveness. This is what matters most. I challenge you to take a moment and ask yourself what could forgiveness do for you? Will you be able to move on, will it make you stop checking his social media, will you be able to have peace and less anxiety? Remember this is for YOU. Also consider what you need to make forgiveness happen. What you need has to be within your control. You can't say that you need him to apologize, or for him to leave the girl he cheated with. If you wait for this, you could be waiting your entire life. Consider what you need to make forgiveness happen. Maybe you need an accountability partner to hold you accountable to forgiveness. Maybe you need a mirror to look into every night and remind yourself what doors forgiveness will open up for you. Maybe you need a support group. Maybe it's building up and restoring your self-esteem and confidence. Whatever you need, take time to uncover that and work to make it happen so that you can get through this journey. Know that forgiveness is the key to moving forward, but it's well within your reach.

Embracing Change
"Incredible change happens in your life when you decide to take control of what you do have power over instead of craving control over what you don't."
— Steve Maraboli

The only constant in the world is change. Life will always have ups and downs and throw things your way that you're not 100% prepared for. It is not personal we all experience change- both good and bad. When we come to understand that, and if we can learn a system to be able to embrace change, then we come out with the success that we desire on the other side.

Transition is a normal part of life. It is estimated that 90% of women are expecting some transition in the next five years. This sort of change can include getting married, starting a family, retirement, becoming an empty nester, divorce, starting a new relationship, etc. Even though some of the most exciting changes come, they can still cause a little bit of tension because, in the end, it's all still new. Change can be overwhelming, so I want to give you a perspective on change so that when it's happening, you're able to grow and not resist it.

There are five stages of change. The five stages are confusion, depression, soul searching, acceptance, and then the new you. Confusion is the beginning stage where you are often trying to figure out what is happening. You will probably ask questions like, "What have I gotten myself into?" Many people get stuck in the state of confusion because it can be paralyzing. It's common to become bitter and question why things are not happening the way that you originally envisioned.

After the confusion stage, you will likely move into the stage of depression. This is a very dark phase where you are often dealing with hurt and pain. Depression is a serious medical condition that negatively impacts your feelings, thoughts, and therefore your actions. You may be dealing with thoughts like "What did I do to deserve this?" or "Why can't my life be normal?" You may also notice changes within yourself, such as isolating from others or losing interest in things that you loved to do. Or, may also notice the complete opposite. Some people get addicted to blocking out the pain. They may overwork themselves, or drown their sorrows in watching too much television.

The truth is that none of those addictions work. Some people develop manic behaviors to cope. They may look for reasons to stay busy or avoid their home, all in an effort to avoid facing the pain. In our society being busy is often looked at as a good thing, but it's not. Blocking out pain doesn't allow you to process. Staying busy and accomplishing things may feel good briefly, but you will never receive long term happiness chasing accomplishments. To move from the depression stage through the remainder of the cycle and into healing, you must be intentional about processing and working through your feelings. I understand, first hand, that working through those emotions can be tough. I know feeling the pain for an extended period of time can feel like torture. I struggled with high functioning depression for years.

From the outside, I looked like I was doing fantastic. I never broke down crying publicly, and I was achieving so many great things back to back. To the outside world it looked like I was adjusting very well to my divorce. The truth is, I was blocking out the things I was dealing with as well as the things I didn't want to confront. As a result of blocking it out, I endured the depression phase for much longer than I needed to. It was terrible for me, both mentally and emotionally. It was not until I was ready to acknowledge what I was feeling, and agree to work through the healing process that I was able to move to the next phase.

The next phase is soul searching. This is where you really start to dig deep and learn more about who you are and what life means for you. This is a major time of reflection. You may begin to ask questions such as "What could I have done differently? Can I be a better person now?" This is where you begin to see the purpose behind your pain. I have seen many clients begin to explore new things about themselves, such as their interests. When I experienced this stage, I became consumed with personal development. I started reading, attending conferences, journaling and I also took a huge step and hired a life coach. I wanted to dig deep into my soul searching and knew that having support during this process would be pivotal to my success.

The soul searching phase looks different for everyone. When you go through a divorce, a lot about your identity and lifestyle changes. For some, you may no longer have your children full time. Maybe your friendships change because they are couples, and you're now no longer tagging along for double dates, etc. For some, it may be a physical move. Understand, while all of the changes are happening and stretching you, you're growing at the same time. Allow yourself to discover who you are. Get to understand the injuries that lie below the insecurities and heal the hurt. When you can do this, you then move to the next and final phase which is acceptance.

The first four phases have really prepared you for this. You come to the point of not blaming other people and yourself for the things that have happened. You begin to accept that this is a part of your story and your testimony, and you can accept it. You might notice yourself feeling a little happier and that you don't indulge in addictions anymore. You may be in a place where you're able to talk about what happened without being ashamed or embarrassed. These indicate that you have come to the point of acceptance. You will notice that your energy is more focused on things that matter, not things that waste your time.

During the acceptance phase, you're combining all of what you learned from the previous stages and defining who you are. This is the stage where you realize that you played small by maintaining a victim mentality, and now you decide to own your power. You realize you can choose to feel happy, you can choose to heal, and you can choose to start the next chapter off well. This is where you begin to work on prioritizing your needs and chose to focus on being happy. Most of us put our happiness into people, into situations, into what we hope for, but the final stage helps you realize that your happiness should not be rooted in anyone else. Happiness is an intentional decision. It is deliberate daily actions that reinforce your desire to be fulfilled and happy.

The stages of change are difficult to go through. Sometimes you will feel like you're doing really well, and then before you know it, you will be set back. Sometimes you may feel like giving up because you feel like you have been in the same stage forever. Do not give up on your healing. If you give up on your healing, you're guaranteed to remain stuck. If you choose to heal you will change your life.

Below the surface
"Below the insecurities are the injuries. Unless you address this, the pain will continue to seep up and cause more hurt."
- Dr. Nicolya

Labeling your divorce will help you become a victim to it or heal it. Have you labeled it a failure? Have you labeled it as something being wrong with you? Have you labeled it trauma? There are many different ways that we identify the situations we experience, which ultimately can impact the way that we view the situation. Take a moment to reflect and consider how you have labeled this divorce. After that, identify how you have been processing and working through it. Have you pushed it under the rug so that nobody notices it? Are you one of those people who will broadcast it on Facebook for attention and sympathy? Or maybe you're an individual that talks to a therapist about it, but when they give you work to do, you never actually implement the work?

When we go through a big transition and things don't go the way that we want them to go, it's easy to push them aside and put our focus onto things that make us feel better. Whether it is binge watching Netflix, shopping with your girlfriends, or oversleeping. These are all things that can be "avoidance tactics" that prevent you from facing the pain.

If you avoid your situation and refuse to process it, you won't face it, and therefore you can't heal. It's like a band aid. You have covered up your pain, but it's still beneath the bandage. Avoidance may feel good in the moment, but ultimately it does not fix the issue. Facing the issue head-on starts with a mindset shift. This is choosing to view the situation from a different lens

Sometimes it's a mental shift, and it does take a lot of work. Earlier in this book we talked about mindset shift and the benefits. Reference that section if you desire to have a total mindset overhaul. Another strategy is to separate yourself from the situation so you can reflect on what is happening and what you're feeling. It also takes away the pressure or idea that something being wrong with you. Many people go through their divorce, but they don't divorce or separate themselves from that part of their story. They wear it like a badge of honor, even though they know it is keeping them stuck, angry, and bitter. I knew of a lady who had been divorced for 20 years and that was her whole identity. She told everyone about, because she had allowed herself to become consumed in this part of her story. No one experience, choice or even mistake can every define you. We are a sum total of all of our experiences and more importantly what we do with them.

I had to learn to separate who I am from my situation. Ultimately I am a single mom, but what would happen if instead of feeling guilt or embarrassment, I just said I am a mother. Yes, you're divorced, but instead of saying, "My name is _____, I am divorced," think about what would change if you were to say, "I am _____. You don't even need to follow it up with your status. It's so sad that society has led us to believe that our wealth, education or relationship status defines us. It does not. There is nothing more or less valuable about you as a single or divorced vs you married. There is often a negative connotation associated with the phrase "single mother" or divorced. I'm divorced, but what if I identify myself as single? I don't have to own that negative connotation of divorce. Instead of saying you're single, you could say you're learning to love yourself or creating new opportunities.

You must learn to separate your identity from the situation. You were not created to carry the burden of guilt and shame. It's taxing on your body, and you deserve more. Learning to separate yourself from that situation can take getting involved with other people who have been through something similar so that they can teach you the process of getting through it.

Failure to detach often results in hiding behind a facade. Have you ever taken a moment to uncover what's underneath the façade? You get your hair and nails done and dress the part to give the image that everything is okay. Below the surface, there are things that are eventually going to start seeping up. It could show up through depression, anxiety, frustration, or irritability. The list goes on, but understand that we are not able to cover those things up for long no matter how good you look on the outside. The human body is made to open up, process, and to learn.

What do you do to get to the root of your pain? The best thing that we can do is to take some time to be alone. I don't mean isolating to the point where you're not allowed to talk to people, you're not allowed to share your story, or you chose to cut people off because you're embarrassed. That's not healthy, and we were made to be in communion with others.

I always ask myself, what can I learn from this? Why is this thought here? I don't want to cover up all of my emotions. Covering up your pain is like shaking a bottle of pop, opening it and expecting it not to explode. Truthfully, when you push it to the back burner, it's still going to come to the forefront at some point. What you're doing is delaying the process and prolonging the pain. When facing the pain sometimes it's healthy to be alone. It is beneficial to take alone time because it helps you to build the emotional and mental stamina you need to push through. Even though it feels painful, it's actually strengthening you because life is going to throw you change time after time, but building the physical and mental stamina to face change is a life skill that will take you very far.

I think that there's a great blessing in being around people, I do believe that we're not always meant to be alone, but I also think there are positive outcomes that can come from being alone. Recently I was on Facebook, and I saw that an artist had drawn a picture of some couples that were lying in bed. They were holding what should have been their phone, but the phone was absent and the whole premise of the article is about how lonely our world really is without the access of social media and phones. We often forget what it means to engage with other people. We keep our minds occupied with Netflix shows and social media among other things.

This article allowed me to reflect on how often we put our energy, effort and thoughts into what other people are doing or making sure we're in constant communication with them. In turn we're missing out on really getting to know ourselves. It is crazy to consider how many people don't know themselves. Sure, you might know your favorite color, favorite food, and you might know what you did as a kid, but do you know deep down what's bothering you? What's hurting you? Do you sincerely know deep down how to heal your heart and your mind? Do you know all that creativity that lies under the surface that you allow to be dormant because of everything else that's going on in life? Do you know how much clarity exists in your world if you shut off the noise? Take a moment and find out.

Conquering your mind
"Happiness depends on your mindset and attitude."
- Roy T. Bennett

During the divorce process, it is so important to be kind to yourself. It's tempting to blame yourself or beat yourself up. The truth is, being mean to yourself has no benefit. Studies show that we have between 12,000-80,000 thoughts a day on average, with women having more thoughts than men. Researchers estimate that 80% of those thoughts are negative. As if that is not bad enough, they believe that 95% of our thoughts are repetitive. So it's like we're replaying negative thoughts over and over. We already know that negative thoughts equal negative emotions and not positive actions. I can't stress this enough: If you can change your mind, you can change your life. The trouble is that changing your mind is not always easy. Recently, I was at the gym with my trainer, and he wanted me to use a hex bar to practice my weighted squats. The bar alone was 60lbs. As I was doing the squats, I felt like I was dying. My trainer felt like it was not challenging enough, so he added 50lbs, 25lbs to each side.

In my mind, I believed that I was barely making it with the hex bar alone, but my trainer saw something in me. He told me that he had watched my form and the way I performed the squats. He explained that he knew I could do it because he believed in me. As I leaned down to pick up the bar, I was feeling a little unsure. I couldn't pick it up. My trainer asked me to stop take a deep breath and get my mind together. He told me, "It's not about your muscles. It's about your mind." He looked at me intently and said, "Do it again. This time, believe you can do it." I leaned down, and would you believe that I did three squats with 110lbs?

The same thing applies in your day-to-day life. If you believe that bad things are coming your way or that divorce has to be viewed in a negative light, then you're going to internalize that. You will then have a repetition of negative thoughts about the situation, and therefore, your actions will match those negative thoughts. My challenge to you is to change your thoughts from seeing divorce as a curse and reframe those thoughts to something positive. Research shows that our world is a reflection of our thoughts. You will see things in a more positive light if you have an optimistic lens from which you are seeing things. When you have a negative outlook, your life will reflect that.

Stop looking at your divorce as something that happened to you or to hurt you. It is something happening for you, for your benefit, for your growth and for your success. What happened to you needed to happen in order for you to find who you need to be. Every time something negative comes your way, think of how you can change the thoughts to something positive. For example, instead of saying, "I can't believe I am divorced. I will never find anyone else to love me." Try saying, "Wow, what new opportunities exist for me after this is over?" Reframing your thoughts will take some time. You have practiced accepting negative thoughts for 20, 30, 40, or even 50 years, depending on how old you are. You must practice breaking that pattern and way of thinking. One of the things I often ask myself concerning my thoughts is, "Is this something I would say out loud to my daughters?" If I think the words "I suck," would I say that to my daughters? Absolutely not. I would never do that, so why is it okay for me to not only say that to myself, but to accept it about myself? You must apply the same concept to yourself.

In addition to reframing your thoughts, it is constructive to start spending more time around positive people. My mom is a very optimistic, glass half full type of person. She can take something so nasty and cynical and really flip it. She always tells me to work on my perspective and my optimism. She believes that her life is positive and happy because she wants it to be and because she believes that in her mind. She shared that she decided to look at it positively and that it has changed her life. My mom had me at 17 and my brother at 18, so as a two-time teen mom, everyone was telling her that she was going to be a statistic. That she would be on welfare and struggle forever. She decided to change her future by changing her actions and thoughts. When I was in fifth grade, she graduated Law School and now is a successful partner in her law firm. She did this as a single teen mom despite how everyone told her this was a curse, and that she would never find success.

Even though we hate to admit it, it's easier to surround yourself with negativity. After all, most of us have normalized it. I notice this when people use support groups in the wrong way. You may be tempted to join a group on Facebook that is titled, "My Ex Sucks." Now you have all these people ranting and raving about how their husband sucks. This may feel good and may feel like a confirmation to your experience, it's also just keeping you in the negative spiral that ultimately doesn't benefit you. I challenge you to find positive people and opportunities so that you continue to reframe those negative thoughts.

Three years ago, I read a book that changed my life. It was called The Miracle Morning by Hal Elrod. It was probably one of the best books I have ever read. The premise of this book is the importance of creating a morning routine that sets you up for success. The author uses an acronym called S-A-V-E-R-S. It breaks down every step that you need to incorporate in your morning to have positive momentum to get through the day. S-A-V-E-R-S stands for Silence, Affirmation, Visualization, Exercise, Reading, and Scribing (which is what we would call journaling). In the morning you can spend 5 to 10 minutes on each. Some people that have long mornings could do 30 minutes on each, but the purpose is to get in the routine of it.

Let's break it down.

Silence is the best way to start your morning. I am a firm believer that most of our problems happen because we are unwilling to sit still with our thoughts. Our days are inundated with things to do, places to go, and people to see. If you can, find five minutes of pure silence before waking and rushing through your day. For some people that may be meditation, for others, it could be prayer. For some people, it is literally the act of being still and silent. You have to incorporate what works for you. I often like to do my silence and scribing back to back. Yes, it breaks up the acronym, but if I am praying or meditating, I like to jot down what comes to my mind. It's a great strategy that has helped me to make sense of all of my thoughts.

Afterward you would do *Affirmations*. Did you know that your subconscious brain doesn't know the difference between reality and what you tell it? Therefore, when you affirm yourself, your subconscious brain will take that as the truth and propel us in the direction that will allow our affirmations manifest. A tangible example I have is when I was writing my first book, one of the affirmations I repeated over and over was, "I, Dr. Nicolya, am a best-selling author." The truth is, I started saying this before I wrote my first word so I was yet even to be an author, let alone a bestselling one. Saying the affirmation every day helped me to remember what I was working towards. Each time I would say it, I would instantly start to consider what I needed to do to make that affirmation come true. Whether it was to contact a cover designer, write, edit or promote, I took action because I wanted that affirmation to be true. My subconscious mind already believed it to be so.

Sometimes when I work with people, they'll say I've been repeating affirmations over and over, but nothing is working. There are a couple of strategies and ideas I'd like to share with you. Our subconscious brain can only take in about 5-10 affirmations at a time, so you don't need to have 30 affirmations. I'd say 5-10 is probably good. Another thing about affirmations is that they do nothing if you say them and then make a statement or have a thought that is contrary to the affirmation. If I say, "I, Dr. Nicolya am happily moving forward creating a life I love" but then follow up with that by laughing at myself or saying that it could never happen, I have now taken a positive statement and affirmation and replaced it with a negative one. I negated the affirmation that I desire to accomplish.

I challenge you to say the affirmations with confidence and hold tight to the faith that they'll come true. Sometimes my daughters will draw affirmations and as they're coloring it they will keep repeating it with increasing levels of emphasis on the affirmation. I joined them recently and I realized this activity helps to solidify it. This covers the last letter "S" for *scribing*. I am doing both affirmation and scribing together this way. Lastly, when you're speaking your affirmations, it is beneficial to say them first thing in the morning and right before bed so that your brain is continually reflecting on that throughout the day and overnight while you are asleep. I actually recorded myself saying my affirmations and will play them for myself. This helps me to think about these affirmations regularly.

The next part of the acronym is *Visualization*. Some people like to announce their vision so that people will watch as it unfolds; however, this puts tremendous pressure on you to accomplish what you have shared. Some people like vision boards where they create their ideal life and goals and put it on a poster board. It serves as a visual reminder on what they are working toward. I have a vision board that I look at every single morning. I also share my goals with those closest to me. However, you desire to announce or layout your vision, the goal is to make it a daily practice to both think about your vision and reflect on it.

Exercise is the next step. Doing a short workout early in the morning revs your metabolism and helps you to focus more on the activities ahead. You don't necessarily need to break a sweat, but you could do a brief Pilates or yoga routine. Sometimes I connect my exercise and the last step of reading together, by reading while exercising on my recumbent bike.

Finally, the last letter is for *Read*. I love reading fiction books, but for the most part, when I'm doing my morning routine, I am ensuring that I'm reading things that are going to educate me. I maximize my reading time by intentionally reading material that will help me grow. This is a great way to start working on your personal development and growth while starting your day off on the right foot.

The mind is something that is challenging to accept. Even scientists disagree on the nature of the mind and matter. However, you don't need to understand everything. You just need to know enough to further yourself and know how you operate, so you can get to where you need to be. I genuinely believe that if you can control and change your mind, you can change your life. When going through a divorce, many people wonder how to heal their mind. After all, there are a lot of thoughts, emotions, and ideas that come up.

One of the greatest ways to better understand the mind is to read. There are many amazing books that have been written on divorce and healing. But it is also good to read a wide variety of literature. Read on topics that you want to learn more about in this stage of your life. It helps to keep your mind learning and active.

Meditation is also a great way to understand your mind better and work on making changes as necessary. Meditation is the art of observing your thoughts. It is the quickest and most widely recognized way to understand your mind. Even if you are incredibly intelligent and successful, the ability to stand outside yourself is necessary for progress. Otherwise, the same habits and tendencies will simply keep repeating themselves.

If you desire insight into your mind, I challenge you to pay attention to your emotions. Much has been said about the power of the mind in terms of generating our reality. Our feelings are a response to whether we are happy or sad with our current environment in a sophisticated real-time feedback system. Emotions have been brushed aside as illogical tendencies, which is a drastic mistake. If you feel bad, it is time to change your thoughts and your situation quickly. Over time, you will gain experience concerning how intricate the emotional system is and how it can serve to guide your thoughts.

Here are several strategies that will help you to conquer your mind and find the peace that you deserve.

- **Avoid obsessing about completely silencing the mind.** You may wish that you could stop your thoughts altogether. However, this isn't the best tactic for dealing with overthinking. The more you try to stop overthinking the more those negative thoughts will flow.
- **Understand that you'll always have thoughts.** Everyone has thoughts. Recognize this is a normal process. Although you can learn to silence your mind in certain situations, you can achieve great peace by learning to take control of *what* you think, instead.
- **Avoid judging your thoughts.** It's tempting to get upset if you have negative thoughts or emotions. You may be quick to judge and try to squash them. Instead of judging and criticizing your thoughts, accept them for normal human emotions. Acknowledge them and then move on. Learn to love your mind because it has been strong enough to get you this far.
- **Try to stay present.** Overthinking often comes because you're worried about the future or regret something that has already happened. YOU CANNOT CONTROL YOUR FUTURE, no matter how hard you think or worry about it. This will only cause you to live in a constant state of fear. If you stay in the present moment, then fear won't take over, and you can spend your time on what you can control in the present.

Your thoughts can save you, but they can also destroy you. Your mind can be a busy place, so it's important to learn ways to deal effectively with some of the thoughts. Strategies like these can help you deal with your overthinking so you can find peace.

Setting goals for your future self
"The relationship you have with yourself is the longest relationship you will have. What are you doing to make that worthwhile?"
-Dr. Nicolya

Many people set out to be the best version of themselves or to be successful, but then they never take that next step to invest in themselves. Whether that's investing money, time, or energy, many people do not see the value with investing. We will spend money, time and energy on clothes, home décor, cars, our kids etc., but not ourselves. I have learned the hard way that if you don't first take care of yourself you're not good to anyone else.

I am a big advocate that you should never set too many goals at the same time because you'll likely get overwhelmed and throw in the towel. Research proves that setting too many goals is the contributing reason to why we fall short. Whenever you're working on growth, you should set approximately two to three goals max. It is important at this time to pick the areas that are most important to you. It may be a physical move, a career move, improvement of finances, or starting a business.

Have you ever heard of P-U-S-H goals? P-U-S-H stands for Positive, Uplifting, Strategic, and Hard. I have heard people talk about this concept regarding goals in business, but I use it a little differently. This is an acronym that I use with my clients, my daughters, and myself that helps us all to remember what we're working towards. The premise of PUSH goals by my definition is that these goals are pushing you beyond your comfort zone to accomplish the things that you desire to get done. PUSH goals press you beyond what you're used to. They push you beyond what you're familiar with. I always say that when a "pause" occurs in life, it's an opportunity to push. What I mean is, when things happen in life that throw us off course or force us to pay attention, these are the very situations that are creating space for us to PUSH past our comfort zone and into growth territory. These are experiences that are giving us permission to reflect and learn. Too many of our actions are simply done out of habit, routine, and rituals that we have created. We have to learn to do things intentionally and not out of habit.

There are three types of habits. There are positive habits, negative habits, and neutral habits. An example of a positive habit would be waking up 20 minutes before your alarm clock to implement a morning routine that sets you up for success—or maybe journaling your feelings before posting them on social media. An example of a negative habit would be sharing all of your personal business on social media. Now, neutral habit is a little more difficult to define, but it is something that is neither positive nor negative. It is just a habit. Some people might put their socks on before their pants. That would be an example of a neutral habit because it doesn't matter if you put your pants on and then your socks or your socks and then your pants. Some people shower at night, and some people shower in the morning. There's no right or wrong time to do it. When it comes to being a successful goal setter, the best thing you can do is better understand your habits, where they come from, and why you do them.

You then want to identify the negative habits that you have. This is important because negative habits can impact the level of success you have in achieving your goals. When you're able to identify the negative habits, you can identify how to avoid them. The best way to stop a negative habit is to replace it with something positive. If your negative habit is to say mean things about yourself, the thing to replace it with is positive affirmations. If your habit is watching television, you may choose to read. The goal is to get rid of bad habits and implement choices that benefit you in the long run.

I know that goal setting does not seem to be related to divorce, but the reality is that when you decide you want to heal, you're setting a goal to heal. Beyond that, you will want to set goals for your new beginning. When you take time to reflect on the things you desire to change in your life after your divorce, you should set a goal. This practice is very much related to the healing process after a divorce. Goal setting is should generally be a part of your life. You should consistently be setting goals that are pushing you outside of your comfort zone.

Regularly you should be setting goals that are going to make you a better version of yourself. I read a statistic that said that 83% of people don't even have goals, 14% of people have goals, but they don't know what to do with them, and then 3% of people have the goal physically written down. The truth is when we haven't identified what we desire out of life, we go through life confused, overwhelmed, and frustrated. When you don't have a map or directions for where you are going, you might not end up there. Create a plan. Confusion costs and clarity saves. Without increasing the clarity in your life regarding what you desire to accomplish and what you hope to feel, you're consistently going to be in a state of frustration. Anyone who knows me knows I recognize that setting and working towards my goals have been my savings grace. This is why I wrote *The Goal Getter Guide* to help other people realize how life changing and valuable goals really are.

There was a study at Harvard Business School where researchers decided that they were going to interview their graduating class to see who had goals. The graduates took turns identifying their goals. Ten years later, they followed up to see where the students were in regards to accomplishing their goals. They found that 3% of that graduating class was more successful than the 97% combined. The researchers were fascinated to see what was different about this group of successful students. In the process of digging deeper to complete their research, they found that 3% wrote down their goals. The other group had goals but did not write them down, and they weren't taking action on them. Therefore, they were not reaching their target because ultimately, they had no clue where they were aiming for. So think about it. If you set no goals after your divorce, it is highly likely that you will remain in a bitter and broken state. If you set the intention to heal and work with a coach and improve self-care, you are more likely to move in a positive direction.

As for the original categories that are represented with P-U-S-H goals, the first step is you want to set a goal that is POSITIVE. It sounds like common sense, but sometimes we set goals thinking they are positive, but they are, in fact, hurtful. For example, if you set a goal to get a boyfriend within the next month, that's likely not a positive goal. Your focus will be on getting a boyfriend and not healing. Therefore, you will be rushing and likely settling for something that is not healthy for you. You need to set a goal that gives you something to look forward to and adds positivity and a benefit to your life.

After this, you want to ensure that your goal is UPLIFTING. This means that the goal should encourage you, motivate you, and inspire you. We often set goals, because that is what other people want for us. Ultimately there is no benefit to you if you are not setting goals that excite and encourage you.

Next, you want the goal to be realistic and STRATEGIC to what you have going on in your life, but also strategically setting you up for success. For example, if you set a goal to move next month because you desperately want to avoid being in the same state as your ex, but you're struggling financially, this may not be a realistic goal. It may be a better idea to set a goal to move within the state with the next month, then set goals that will position you to move out of state. Once you identify that the goal is realistic, now you can identify the strategy to make it happen.

Finally, the goal needs to be HARD. Do not set goals that are comfy or familiar. I see women do this too often and sell themselves short. Set a goal that is going to PUSH you because that is where you are going to grow. Staying in a familiar and comfortable place will not help you to grow. In fact, that is the very thing that keeps you stuck. Growth is what you need during this time; don't run from it.

I remember going through my divorce and decided that my PUSH goal would be to write my first book. This goal was extremely positive because it was something that would add value to my life. The goal was uplifting because, despite what was going on, it gave me something to look forward to and work toward. In regards to strategic, I laid out a list of pros and cons of writing a book. By far, the biggest advantage was the fact that I would have a chance to write, which was an outlet, but also a chance to change other's lives as well. I knew that being a single parent was tough and that I would need to have a lot of time to be available to my children who were also hurting during this time. So I laid out a detailed strategy for incorporating book writing, editing and marketing into my daily schedule. This process was indeed very hard. I had never written a book, and I did not have anyone around me who had. During my time of reflection, I was able to see that this was indeed a PUSH goal, so I decided to go after it.

PUSH goals can be tough to balance because they are usually difficult and push you beyond your comfort zone. After you identify your top two to three PUSH goals, start working backward from the goal you identified. Break the goal down into reasonable steps. Start with the daily steps you need to take that equal the big goal. Identify the small steps that can be done daily, then do the same for weekly steps, then monthly. For example, I wanted to write a book to get my name out into the business world. As a part of my daily steps, I wrote for an hour each day. My weekly steps included different things such as contacting editors, designers and creating posts for social media to promote my book. My monthly steps were to find venues for book signings as well as interviewing other authors for insight. This took a once overwhelming PUSH goal and made it more manageable. When you make the goal more manageable, it feels like it is within your reach, and in turn, you're less likely to give up on the target.

You can do the same thing for healing. Imagine that you decide that you want to go out and find a support group, but battle with social anxiety. This is indeed a PUSH goal and one I can very much relate to as an introvert. You may give yourself one month to find and join a group. Your daily goal may be to research groups. Your weekly goal may be to visit one group per week. Finally, by the end of the month, you have information to make an informed decision and join a group. As you can see, it started off as a BIG goal, but you made it manageable.

When you break your goal down into bite-size chunks, it also allows you to reflect on your progress regularly as well. For example, if during your marriage you gained a lot of weight, but now decide that you want to be healthy and live in a body you love, you may set a goal to work out for an hour four days per week. Each week you may decide to reflect on how you are doing in regards to the four-hour goal. If you notice each Tuesday you're missing your fitness class because it clashes with your son's football practice, maybe you decide that Tuesdays aren't the day and you need to join a class on Wednesday instead.

Maybe you realized you're missing the class because you're staying up too late and not responding to your alarm clock. You may decide that you will DVR your show and catch it the next day instead of staying up late. The point is you want to reflect on the goal regularly to be able to address your progress accurately. When we set BIG goals, many people miss the importance of reflecting; therefore, they do not make much progress with their goals. When you break the goal into bite-size chunks, then you have a better grasp on what you should be doing daily, weekly, and monthly.

Trust me, I know that transitions can cause a lot of tension and chaos, and ultimately can be an emotional barrier that gets in the way of you thinking that you deserve anything more. But do not allow your situation to fool you. You do deserve more. Setting goals allows you that opportunity to have something to look forward to. It's a great reminder that life is valuable and that life is worth living. I want you to set a goal that you are so passionate about that it keeps you up at night and smiling during the day. Commit to it over the next 90 days.

Redefining who you are
"Every day you reinvent yourself. You're always in motion. But you decide every day: forward or backward."
-James Altucher

After going through a divorce, many people lose themselves. One of the hardest things to do, but most needed is to learn to redefine who you are. Instead of getting caught up in confusion and frustration, you have to take some time for real reflection. Who are you without your soon-to-be ex-husband? Who are you without the title at corporate? Who are you at the core of your being? Are you strong? Are you powerful? Are you motivational? Are you encouraging? Are you shy? It is tempting to limit yourself, but when you do that, you limit future possibilities.

Take some time to highlight your values and what matters to you. What are the things that you're passionate about, your desires, your hopes? Take a moment to see who you are without the pain, hurt, failures and frustrations. I have worked with clients who make extreme changes after their divorce. It's not because they are going crazy or through a mid-life crisis, but because the divorce helped them to see things differently. The divorce gave them a chance to find themselves. Their divorce made them see how they have lived a watered-down version of themselves.

I have seen clients make simple changes, such as trying to get back into cooking and incorporating new cooking recipes into their life. On the other end, I have witnessed clients leave a corporate job to pursue a dream of starting an interior decorating business. Working that corporate job that made them feel like they were killing their creativity, and they felt trapped. Pain and loss can cause you to notice that life is short and realize how important it is to make the most of it.

I remember a while back, I had this dream of a little boy handing me a blue marker. It did not make sense, but in the dream, he kept handing me the marker. Each time I tried to hand the marker back and explain that I did not want it. The next morning over breakfast, my daughters and I talked about our dreams, and so I decided to share my dream, thinking I was just making conversation. My oldest daughter looked me in my eyes and said, "I know why you had that dream. It's because sometimes you get stuck in one idea, and you're not open to new things. What if God is opening your mind to new and creative things?"

Her response hit me like a ton of bricks because although the dream was seemingly insignificant and felt random, the truth is I was really closed off to new things. I had a routine and ritual and was truly closed off to new ideas because it felt like it was going to interrupt my system. I had created a very detailed and organized routine because truthfully, my life felt like it was spinning out of control with the divorce. I knew at that moment that I needed to open my heart and my mind to new things.

There's so much excitement when it comes to change, and I think that, unfortunately, we focus on the things we don't want regarding the change. We place our focus on the things that are frustrating and overwhelming us when instead, we should be embracing change and choose to focus on the positive things that can come from it.

There are a lot of new changes that come with divorce. Instead of trying to avoid them, we can shift our perspective. How can you celebrate the new beginning instead of allowing bitterness, anger, irritability, and frustration to take over your life? How can you look at this change in a positive way and decide to be intentional about embracing this new opportunity? I want you to remember that change is not personal. It happens to all of us, but the greatest thing about it is that if you choose to look at your change with an optimistic lens, it will be easy to see the benefits.

After going through a divorce, it can be embarrassing to acknowledge what you're going through, but to need help with it can be even more uncomfortable. Therefore, it is not always easy to ask for the help you need and desire. Here are ways that you can ask for help or support without sounding desperate.

- **Be honest with yourself.** Sometimes we want support so we can allow ourselves to stay in a victim mentality. If this is the case, you have to be honest with yourself and note that this is not a good place to remain. Chose instead to get help so that you can work towards healing in a healthy way.
- **Make your request specific.** Saying you need help can look different for each situation. Do you need someone to help babysit your children once per week, or check on you, or plan an outing? Identifying exactly what you need lets the other person know if they can support you with that need.
- **Pay attention to your emotions.** There are going to be times where you desire to be alone and times where you want to be with people. Pay attention to your body, because it will always tell you what you need.

- **Know who to ask for help.** If you're looking for support for your divorce from your ex-mother-in-law, that is likely not the best person to ask. Consider talking and getting support from people who are not in any way impacted by your divorce, such as a coach and a counselor. Also, do not attempt to get support from a new relationship. It is unhealthy to bring forth your problems, hurts, and concerns when you're trying to begin something new. This can create a whole host of problems.
- **Do not assume.** While your best friend may want to help you she may not be emotionally available or she may not even understand how to support you. Before assuming you can ask certain people for support, make sure they are open and willing to be supportive to you.
- **Do not take it personally if someone can't do it.** This gives you a chance to get support from others who are more willing and emotionally able to give you the support you need.

What I want you to understand is that just because you're divorced or going through a divorce, it doesn't mean that something is wrong with you. In fact, it means the total opposite. It means you're strong enough to know what you need and deserve and to create an opportunity that allows for you to go after it. That is something that most people never know.

Self-love
"The best gift you can ever give yourself is unconditional love. After all, you deserve it."
~Dr. Nicolya

After going through a divorce, your self-worth will probably take the biggest hit. This includes self-esteem, self-love, and self-care. Sadly, I don't feel like enough of us truly understand the benefits of self-love. I have to admit that I'm still recovering from all of the behavior that I adopted and accepted as normal, which prevented me from loving myself. I am passionate about teaching other people to be able to do the same thing now.

Self-love is such a dynamic concept. It continuously grows, and the more we practice it, the more it teaches other people not only how to treat us but how they should be treating themselves. Self-love is a great concept, but there are not enough people implementing it. Recently, I was talking to a client, and I was asking her if she felt like she loved herself. She proceeded to tell me all of the things that she bought for herself as well as the things that she did for herself. The vacation she took, the shoes she bought, the massage benefits that she had. What I shared with her is what I'm going to share with you: If you believe that you love yourself based on the material things you have attained, then your self-love is non-existent.

Many people believe that self-love equates to being selfish. It's as if we're supposed to be selfless and love other people and treat other people better and put ourselves on the back burner. Society has this expectation that we're supposed to be superhuman and do everything for everyone else. The definition of being selfish is to be inconsiderate, thoughtless, egocentric, and self-absorbed. These words do not at all match the concept of self-love. Self-love is about being unapologetically you, taking responsibility for yourself with all your imperfections, flaws, and even the things that you're embarrassed about. Self-love is about respecting yourself, knowing who you are, and having boundaries for yourself to ensure that you are being treated appropriately. If you are wondering if you're struggling with self-love, here are some signs that you may be struggling with it.

- **Making choices that you regret.** Sometimes you know you're going to regret them before you make them. These choices often put you in situations where you're giving too much.
- **You lack boundaries.** Maybe you're not sure who you are, what you want, or you just go through life living based on what other people tell you should be

doing. Maybe you get stuck in unhealthy or unhappy relationships or toxic relationships, you probably have no time for fun, or you often feel guilty when not working or doing something productive.
- **You believe and say mean things about yourself.** Maybe you only feel valuable if you're dressed up or if someone compliments you, but deep down you don't really feel or believe it.

To incorporate self-love, it would mean you need to sacrifice and change things about yourself, your life, and your habits. But increasing self-love would also equal the opportunity for you to have the ability to embrace change. It'll be a chance for the opinions and thoughts of others to hold no value or less value altogether. You would have a greater level of confidence, self-esteem, and you would have an improvement in your overall well-being. The question that you're here to answer and wanting to understand better is how do you go about increasing self-love.

The first step to increasing self-love comes from Stephen Covey's book, The 7 Habits of Highly Effective People. This is the habit of doing your "have to's" before your "want to's." Sometimes you may do things because they feel better in the moment. You may stay busy because if you sit still with your thoughts, it will hurt. The reality is that when you go out and drink with friends because it's to avoid going home and facing the fact that you need to get your budget done, only to discover that you've overspent. This can leave you feeling regret and resentment. This makes it difficult for you to love yourself because you may be offended or disappointed as a result of your actions and experiences. You must identify the critical tasks and prioritize those things in your life. The next step is to practice mindfulness. Having the ability to be still incredibly important. You may try to negotiate with yourself concerning the things in your past, to justify why you weren't able to exercise self-love.

The truth is while we would love to change the past and the future, we have no control of either. The only thing we have control over is our here and now. Therefore, we must practice mindfulness by staying in the moment and maintaining focus. Being still with our thoughts is important because we can learn from our thoughts, and more importantly, we can shift or change them at any given time. So, no, we may not be able to change the past or future, but we can take steps and make choices that will have a positive impact on our future. This is why mindfulness is such a critical component.

The next step is to build your self-esteem. This is a critical component of self-love. As I think about myself as I went through my divorce journey, I had to learn who I was. There was a period in time when I rushed that healing process, but once I slowed down, I was able to see the losses. I was able to be patient in learning what I needed, and through that, it built the resilience. The next time something came up, I was able to tackle it more effectively because I was confident in my approach based on what I learned from my previous experience.

Another element of having self-love is having a healthy level of self-esteem. If you feel good about yourself, it will impact your overall mental health and, in turn, increase your self-love. So what is self-esteem? It's what you see and think about yourself. Self-esteem is driven by the confidence you gain as you experience life and relationships. Each of those experiences either adds or removes from the value you see in yourself. This makes me think back to a situation early in my life. When I was a little girl, I loved singing and was confident about it. One time, I sang in front of a good friend of mine, but she told me I sucked as a singer. This response tore my self-esteem to shreds. To this day, I struggle with singing in front of people. When I was in college, someone told me that they thought I was pretty good with organization and productivity and that they needed my help. They needed my help organizing and balancing all of their classes. As a result of their need for help, it built my confidence in that area. I dug myself into that and made it a priority. Now I do it for a living.

Notice, those are two different experiences that molded my self-esteem in different ways. So ask yourself: "What is my self-esteem made of? What experiences in my life have contributed to and taken away from my self-esteem?" The negative impacts of low self-esteem are no fun. People with low self-esteem often don't believe in themselves. They see themselves as failures before they even begin, so usually, they won't start anything. People with low self-esteem also have a hard time forgiving their mistakes and tend to dwell on them for a very long time. They can never truly love themselves and, in turn, cannot truly heal.

People with low self-esteem are often afraid to show their true selves. They believe that people will judge them or people won't really like them, and so they often put on this façade to pretend to be somebody who they're not. I can't stress this enough, but pretending to be somebody that you're not is one of the most exhausting things that you can ever do. It is so exhausting to keep up that façade continually. The reality is that it's okay to be unique and embrace yourself. It's okay to allow yourself to learn from that, to allow yourself to recognize who you are. We are all made to have unique qualities and experiences because it's what makes us who we are. People with high self-esteem don't worry about rejection or acceptance. They just embrace who they are. They often dare to express themselves openly, honestly, and with confidence. It also creates inspiration. When I openly share the story of what I've gone through, a lot of people are drawn to that and want to learn because that's not something that most people do. It's kind of seen as outlandish or different. But when you build that self-esteem, you have the courage to be yourself and be okay with it.

Afterwards, in regards to self-love is setting boundaries for yourself and others. When self-love is lacking, so are boundaries; When this happens, situations, places and people will exhaust you. Every time that you over commit to somebody else that is the time you're taking something away from yourself. Also, with regards to boundaries, we should not only set them with others, but with ourselves as well. So, you know those late nights when you want an extra cookie, but then you wake up feeling guilty because you're putting on weight or you don't feel good about yourself? Or the night that you know you need sleep because you're not effective or productive at work, but you stay up late and watch another episode of your favorite show because that feels good. You have to create and set boundaries and make them a regular practice to show in order to value yourself. When you don't have boundaries in place, you allow yourself to believe that the things that you need and deserve don't matter and that you shouldn't get them.

The next step to self-love is to consider your thoughts. How is your thought life? I hate to break it to you but our life is a reflection our thoughts. When you think negative things, your life is going to reflect that. So, take a moment and consider the things you think of yourself. Do you hate yourself? Are you mad at yourself?

Do you not love yourself? Are you frustrated with yourself? If you're feeling all of these, your outer actions will reflect that, and it will become difficult to love yourself. I always tell my clients that the reality is the world will knock us down, there will always be someone who's not happy with the way we look, the way we act, the choices we've made, who we are, and so many other things. The truth is, you have to be your own cheerleader, so when the world is not in agreement, you're still in the background believing in yourself and cheering yourself on. A big part of that is self-forgiveness. The bible tells us that God works everything together for the good of those who love him. It is important to understand that because self-forgiveness is sometimes tricky when you're frustrated with where you are in life. If you can shift your perspective, you can embrace the perspective that everything happens for a reason and that you know it's all a part of the plan. All of your experiences are a part of creating you into who you're supposed to be.

The final step is to live intentionally. I often notice when I work with new clients that so many people are living life by default by allowing life to happen, then responding to it. You do not have to allow things to just happen to you. You have a right to design your life. When you live by default, you're always going to be at the mercy of other people's situations. We have to recognize that we have power in the way in which we respond to our experiences in life. Not only is it important to have the knowledge, it's more important to have the strength and courage to step into that power. It's imperative that you choose to live by design and not by default.

Now, when you think of self-love, you're likely wondering what that looks like. Practical self-love strategies would look like starting each day by telling yourself something positive. This could be in the form of affirmations. It could also be starting your day with gratitude, or honing in and focusing on the positives instead of the negatives that are happening in your life. In addition, a self-love strategy is going into environments where you're wanted and not tolerated. I struggled with this for years. I went into places (work, social events etc.) because I felt like I needed to be there, but I could tell it wasn't healthy. Sometimes they were flat out toxic. Sometimes people would talk down towards me when they heard all my goals. I remember when I first got my doctorate, a colleague told me that I changed my title to cover up the fact that I was no longer married.

These were the type of people that I would be around because I didn't love myself enough to know that I deserved healthy friendships. I didn't even have the confidence or self-love to defend myself by saying how hurtful that was. I didn't even really understand what a healthy friendship looked like until I started to love myself. Surround yourself with the people who love, encourage, inspire you, and believe in you.

A practical self-love strategy I use regularly is to stop the comparison. This is so difficult in this day and age because of social media. I recently had an experience at the gym, and my trainer had me lunging around the track. At first, it felt good because I could feel my muscles working. Then I started to keep discouraged as I was going around the track because I realized that I was going slowly compared to the people on the outer part of the track. They were running faster around me. Now, logically I know that they were running, and I was lunging, so there's no way I could keep up the same pace with them. It was somewhat discouraging though, because it didn't feel like I was effective. What I realized is that I was spending too much time focusing on the people on the other end of the track instead of focusing on my unique race. I immediately had to reframe my thinking and remember that my own goal. We have different experiences for different reasons. It is important that we aren't constantly comparing ourselves to other people our goal and our focus should be on our own journey and in our own lane to help us to be successful. If we put all of our energy and effort into other people, we lack the energy and effort we need to succeed.

An additional strategy is to get in touch with your inner dialog. I think the biggest problem with humankind is the unwillingness to be still with ourselves. Anytime we have downtime, we want to fill it with something else. Whether that's calling a friend, being on social media, listening to a podcast, going to sleep, watching a TV show, staying busy at work, or running errands, it's always something. When we remove these distractions and are able to sit still, that's when we can really learn who we are, we can learn about our needs, our desires, and our struggles. We can learn what we need to move forward and to succeed. There are so many different things we can learn in choosing to be still. We can learn the areas where were stuck and how to tackle those obstacles. So, learn to be okay with sitting still. I implemented a practice to sit still for ten minutes a day. For others, this could be practicing yoga or meditation. So many things would start to flood my mind. What I came to see is that while checking off my to-do list, it wasn't getting me any closer to my internal dialog, or who I am at my core. If you're running from the need to sit still, that is proof that you need to be still with yourself and, more importantly, something you need to be learning from.

An important practical self-love strategy is to be patient with yourself. You can sometimes find yourself getting frustrated with seeing other people experience the result we believe we should have when they go through a similar situation. You must be patient through the process. This is where you can really learn to explore more about yourself. When you take that time to do that, you build the skills and the resiliency you need to move forward.

The final example is to celebrate you. Who are you below the façade? Who are you below the hurt? Celebrate every part of you, every flaw and all the beautiful, the ugly, the good, and the bad. The reality is that there is no one else like you, and that is your power; that is your gift.

Self-care is an important part of self-love as well. Self-care is an activity that we do deliberately to take care of our mental, emotional, and physical health. Self-care is a key to improving your mood, reducing your anxiety, and also to having healthier relationships with other people. A lot of times, we confuse the idea of self-love and self-care because self-love and self-care sound similar. While the two falls under the same umbrella, the truth is self-care is a key component of self-love.

So, while self-love is regard for your own well-being and your happiness, self-care is taking care to improve your overall well-being. Self-love is being present with your body, while self-care is doing something your body says it needs or something your body's asking for. Self-love is taking responsibility for your life, while self-care is taking care of yourself. Self-care is like the physical steps that you need to take while self-love is the inner healing; that's the best way I can describe it.

For years, I indulged in many different self-care practices as a way of taking care of myself. I signed up for massages, I would get my nails done, I would take vacations but what I learned through this practice is that I was still emotionally struggling. That's when I learned about the importance of self-love because self-love is about being able to love each and every part of yourself, not just taking care of the parts of yourself that people can see. Self-love is being able to sit quietly with yourself and exist without tension or frustration. Deep down it is about truly connecting with yourself.

Self-care reduces the negative effects of stress. Self-care is a great strategy when you're dealing with a lot of pressure. It also helps to make you more productive, and contributes to your overall well-being physically, mentally, and emotionally. So, practical self-care strategies look like making sleep a part of your daily routine, eating well, doing things you enjoy, moving your body, etc. At the conclusion of this book is a bonus self-care review. I highly suggest you take some time to commit to working through it to review your self-care strategies thoroughly. Also, I suggest you commit to implementing some of the self-care activities in the review section. Trying out new self-care activities can be good for your overall well-being, but is especially important during the healing process.

Now, I want you to take a moment to think of somebody in your life that you love very much. Is it your children? Your parents? Is it a friend? Who was a person that you love so much you would never wish anything bad on them? Who is the person you think about all the time and pray for? Who is the person you have nothing but love for? Now, I want you to consider how you treat them. Take some time and reflect on this honestly. Now consider this: Are these the same things that you are doing to and for yourself? Are you treating yourself in the same manner that you would treat them? When you identify your person, I doubt you run them ragged. I am pretty sure you don't say mean things about them or to them. I am sure you do not beat them up or knock down their confidence when you get a chance. I am close to positive that you're not putting them on the back burner. So why would you treat yourself in that manner?

This reflection practice highlights the need for self-love. The belief is the more you love yourself, the more you're capable of loving others. This activity allows you to learn a lot about your need for self-love and what self-love should look like for you based on how you're showing it to other people. Make it a priority that you step into your power, acknowledging that you are unique, and that is the most special part about you. Make it a priority that you learn to love yourself because, ultimately, the relationship you have with yourself is the longest relationship you will ever have. Choose self-love. Learn to love every part of yourself so that you can effectively move through life, have more success, have more confidence, have more peace, and have more enjoyment.

Conclusion
"Moving forward doesn't equal forgetting. It means choosing to be happy instead of hurt."
-Dr. Nicolya

Marriage is a beautiful thing, and then one day, it's not. When you're getting married, it's so exciting, and you have tons of people excited for you. When you're divorcing, it's a very lonely place to be. Some people believe that marriages take a lot of work while I agree, the truth is divorce takes even more work. It is not the easy way out as many assume. The work in a marriage is rewarding because you have a strong relationship and supportive partner to do life with. Some may believe that the work in divorce is exhausting and not rewarding. But if you do it right, the work you put in through your divorce is rewarding because, ultimately, it can change your life.

Divorce is indeed one of the most painful things an individual can go through. It's not only the death of a marriage but also the end of dreams and hopes. The truth is that the healing or recovery process may not be easy, but it sure beats staying in the valley of despair. Now with the internet having thousands, maybe even millions of statistics regarding divorce, it's no wonder that people become consumed in those stats. Going through my divorce allowed me the opportunity to learn a lot, instead of looking at statistics and then beating myself up because I became one. I would view divorce as a chapter in my life to learn and grow from. I found four perspectives during my divorce that I now hold to.

Change is nature's way of telling us that something is broken and needs to be fixed. If you're able to acknowledge the pain, then you can take steps to work through it. With all loss, there are many emotions such as hurt, anger, guilt, and deep grief- all of which need to be expressed; otherwise, they will be acted out destructively. Nothing lasts forever, not even pain. So know that you won't feel this way for the rest of your life. With divorce, it is common to feel that life is over or that nothing good will ever happen again. However, if you work through the recovery process, the pain will pass, and you can come out as a much healthier person.

When we go through difficult experiences, the best thing we can do for ourselves is to learn from it. When you open your mind to learning from your experience, you will come to see that the divorce did not happen to you, it happened for you. The greatest way we can use our pain is to allow it to motivate us to grow and then support others who are going through similar trials. I use my own experience and testimony to support women and remind them that they're not alone, which reminds me every day that my pain was not in vain. I always say that my divorce broke me, but from that broken place God rebuilt me. So while I was angry and hurt it happened, many of things I am doing now could have never taken place had I not had that experience.

At any given moment, we have two options. We can choose to step forward into growth or to fall back into safety. I suggest moving towards growth because your comfort zone doesn't have anything good waiting for you. The longer you hold tight to the past, the more it will hurt. Remember, your future needs you much more than your past. I know that this time is difficult. It can be especially difficult to believe that peace will come, but ultimately you deserve peace. One strategy I have used to incorporate peace into my life is gratitude. Here is how you can do that too:

- **Search for the positive.** You may be going through a stressful or difficult period in your life, but it shouldn't stop you from seeing positive things. By focusing on the positive aspects of your life, you'll find areas in which you can still feel thankful for. What are the positive areas in your life that aren't being affected by your current challenges? Do you still have your home and health? Do you still have a job that provides for your family? Have you made new friends that can support you or relate to what you are going through.
- **Search for joy.** It's important to add joy to your daily schedule. Watch a comedy, read a comic book, or share jokes with friends. Add laughter to your routine. Joy can help you feel appreciation towards your family, friends, coworkers, and neighbors.
- **Put your pain in perspective.** Make it a point to avoid getting lost in the negative emotions of your challenges by looking at others. If you can put your pain in perspective, you'll discover that you have a lot to offer the world with what you learned and who you're becoming.

Your ability to find gratitude doesn't have to be limited during challenges. Search for the positive areas in your life, even as you struggle in other areas. Remember that you're not alone. Also hold tight to the truth that everything changes. Soon, you'll find yourself feeling gratitude naturally without having to force it.

Don't get caught up in the all or nothing thinking about what you're going through. Don't allow your thoughts to run rampant, causing you to fall prey to negative thoughts that tell you your life is over. Allow your divorce to be the starting point for you, redefining who you are and starting your life over again. While endings are tough to experience, they are also new opportunities if you open your mind to this perspective. Know that there is so much wisdom in your wounds, but you have to allow yourself to discover this. Give yourself a chance to heal. Heal your mind, heal your emotions and, in turn, heal your life.

And most importantly remember you can, and you will survive your split!

BONUS Self-care review
"Self-care is how you take your power back."
-Lalah Delia

When going through a divorce it's tempting to put yourself on the back burner. Now that you know this is no longer an option, if you truly want to heal, I have included this assessment to help you identify strategies for each area of your life that you can implement to take better care of yourself. After completing this, I challenge you to pick three areas where you need to show self-care more regularly and pick one idea from each category that you will begin to implement starting today.

Using the scale below, rate the following areas in terms of frequency:
3= occasionally
2 = Rarely
1= Never
0 = It never occurred to me/ I would not like this

Physical Self-Care

___ Eat regularly (e.g. breakfast, lunch, and dinner)
___ Eat healthy
___ Exercise
___ Get medical care when needed
___ Take time off when needed
___ Do a physical activity that is fun
___ Get enough sleep
___ Wear clothes you like and make you feel and look good
___ Take vacations
___ Take time away from telephones
___ Other:

Psychological Self-Care

___ Take time for self-reflection
___ Have your own personal support system
___ Journal regularly
___ Read something that interests you
___ Set and implement boundaries

___ Be still and notice your inner experience
___ Practice replacing negative thoughts with positive thoughts
___ Engage your intelligence in a new area (e.g. go to an art museum, try learning a new skill)
___ Practice receiving from others
___ Say "no" to extra responsibilities sometimes
___ Other:

Emotional Self-Care

___ Spend time with others whose company you enjoy
___ Stay in contact with important people in your life
___ Give yourself affirmations, praise yourself
___ Love yourself
___ Re-read favorite books, review favorite movies
___ Allow yourself to cry
___ Find things that make you laugh
___ Play with children or visit the elderly
___ Other:

Spiritual Self-Care

___ Read your bible
___ Spend time with nature
___ Go to church
___ Join a spiritual community (like a small group)
___ Be open to inspiration
___ Cherish your optimism and hope
___ Be aware of nonmaterial aspects of life
___ Give back to those in need
___ Identify what is meaningful to you and notice its place in your life
___ Meditate
___ Pray
___ Sing
___ Have experiences of awe and reflect on these
___ Contribute to causes in which you believe
___ Read inspirational literature (talks, music, etc.)
___ Other:

Workplace, Entrepreneurial or Professional Self-Care

___ Take a break during the workday
___ Make quiet time to complete tasks uninterrupted
___ Use your creativity
___ Set boundaries/limits with your clients and colleagues
___ Arrange your work space so it is comfortable and comforting
___ Negotiate for your needs (benefits, pay raise)
___ Develop a non-trauma area of professional interest
___ Other:

Balance

___ Strive for balance within your personal life and your workday
___ Strive for balance among work and family
___ Strive for balance between work and play
___ Strive to find balance between giving to other people and taking care of yourself

www.ingramcontent.com/pod-product-compliance
Lightning Source LLC
Chambersburg PA
CBHW030001050426
42451CB00006B/78